# A Woman's Write:
## Strong and Free

Poetry from Womankind

A Woman's Write:
Strong and Free

Poetry from Womankind

———————— *authors from the* ————————

**WOMANKIND ADDICTION SERVICE**
**CREATIVE WRITING PROGRAM**

iUniverse, Inc.
Bloomington

**A WOMAN'S WRITE: STRONG AND FREE**
**POETRY FROM WOMANKIND**

*iUniverse books may be ordered through booksellers or by contacting:*

*iUniverse*
*1663 Liberty Drive*
*Bloomington, IN 47403*
*www.iuniverse.com*
*1-800-Authors (1-800-288-4677)*

*ISBN: 978-1-4697-3257-2 (sc)*
*ISBN: 978-1-4697-3258-9 (ebk)*

*Printed in the United States of America*

*iUniverse rev. date: 03/27/2012*

# Contents

# About the Program

A Woman's Write: Strong and Free is a compilation of poetry that has been created by the Women's Creative Writing Program at St. Joseph's Healthcare, Womankind Addiction Service in Hamilton, Ontario Canada. The program encourages women to let go of their inhibitions, tap into their creative selves, and feel the sense of empowerment that follows. By losing ourselves in our writing, we are able to access a part of our authentic self and bring it to light in a way that helps us understand who we are and reminds us that we have a voice. We hope you enjoy this book and that it inspires you to find your own hidden writer.

# Class of December 2011

"Writing has opened me up to so many endless possibilities. Words flow through my body with an energy, my fingertips dance with anticipation. My hands begin to tell a story my mouth could not express."

Johanna Cadogan

"Going to writer's group makes me feel liberated. I can clear the cobwebs from my mind and let the pen flow. The writer's group draws out old memories. Some that I cherish and others that need to come to light."

Naomi Jackson

"I never knew I could express my thoughts on paper until I got involved in Womankind. The words just seem to flow on the paper for me."

Susan Castrinos

"Coming to writing class has given me the gift of writing my mind. Focusing on the experiences, feelings, losses, loves, gifts and creativity that live inside me, now I can truly 'see Mary run'. Every class I give a bit more of my true self. I found me at the end of a pen."

Mary Markey

"At 52 I wondered when I would get that thing. What am I here for? At the end of the first writing class my answer was given. When you're not sure you're good at anything, what a pleasure to know that others think you have found your niche. Right or wrong, I'll write the wrong."

Michele Ince

"Thanks to the writer's group, I have unlocked one of the many doors to a whole new world inside of me that I love."

Laura Rooney

# Acknowledgements

A book like this is not created without a lot of special people working hard to make it come true.

Thank you to Debbie Bang for her unwavering support and relentless enthusiasm, providing us a place to flourish, finding the funds and waving the flag.

Thank you to Justine and Andrea who jump in and lead class whenever they're needed—even though their drive is more than an hour and there always seems to be a snowstorm or some other weather demon in the way.

Thank you to the Board of Directors, Susan Clairmont, Chris Roberts, Debbie Bang, Bill Johnston, Emily Clarke, Justine Nicholls, Nancy O'Brien, Nancy Watt and Stephanie McManus who support us unreservedly and enthusiastically (did you know that all of the Board Meetings would be at 7:30 am?).

Thank you to St. Joseph's Hospital for continuing to allow us to express ourselves honestly, uncensored and unguarded.

Thank you to Susan Clairmont, Scott Gardner and The Hamilton Spectator for their continued coverage and support of our program (we think the Spec is the greatest newspaper in Canada!).

Thank you to Bill and Emily for their gentle, intuitive and nurturing editing. You bring out the best in us.

Thank you to Carolyn Leger, an amazing photographer and passionate advocate.

Thank you to April Anderson for sharing your art as well as your writing.

Thank you to the December 2011 authors who provided the quotations. Your work will be featured in our next book. Your warmth, courage and spirit made December the best writing group ever.

Finally, thank you to all of the authors who have made this book a reality. You have shared your authentic self and learned a little more about who you are in the process. It has been an honour to write with you.

Sincerely,
Gail Mercer-MacKay

# Introduction

In life, the authors of this book are recovering addicts. On paper, they are scared and brave. Proud and ashamed. Angry and at peace. In other words, they are a lot like the rest of us.

By writing about their lives and their dependence on drugs and alcohol, these women have invited us to be a part of their journey. They have asked us to share in their struggles and triumphs and to understand that everyone's story matters. Everyone's voice deserves to be heard.

More importantly, writing has allowed these authors to discover themselves. To figure out where they've been and where they want to go.

The women have all—by various routes—come to sit at some point around the table at the Womankind writing program at the Womankind Addiction Service which is part of St. Joseph's Healthcare in Hamilton, Ontario in Canada. Some came and wrote only once. Others came, returned week after week, year after year, and have never stopped writing.

A Woman's Write: Strong and Free is their second book. Their first, called A Woman's Write: A Journey Through Addiction and Recovery was published in 2009.

For the authors, the poems and prose compiled in this book represent a piece of their recovery process. For the reader, they represent some damn fine writing that will make us think and feel.

Susan Clairmont
Columnist
The Hamilton Spectator

(Susan Clairmont wrote a 5-part series on the authors of Womankind. It is available at thespec.com)

# My Name Is . . .

When I look in the mirror,
I see just an outline of my face,
Not yet filled in.
I'm not fully there,
Only a faint description of what I strive to be,
What I want to be.

Where am I?
Will I ever be complete?
Will this outline of my soul be filled with confidence?
Will I be the person I want to be,
Filled with inner peace and happiness?

As I look in the mirror,
A light starts to glow around that face in the mirror.
I close my eyes,
I feel that light on my face and I seem to blossom.
That strong, independent woman thriving for a life,
That's not just an outline.

I see myself.
I see life with potential.
I will not turn away.
I will face my demons and conquer them.
I will use my knowledge learned in treatment.

My name is Sarah and I'm an alcoholic.

Sarah N.

# WRITING

# I Do Not Want To Write

I do not want to write about things I do not want to write about.

I do not want to write about things that hurt too much to think about.

I do not want to write about things that have happened in the past.

I do not want to write about things I've done or things that have been done to me.

I do not want to write about anything that I wouldn't want someone else to read.

I do not want to write about people who are not important to me.

I do not want to write about the things I do not admit to myself.

I do not want to write my secrets,

Secrets about me,

Secrets I keep deep inside of me,

In a dark place I never want to see.

I do not want to write about the things I pretend I do not feel.

I do not want to write about pretending.

I do not want to pretend.

I do not want to write about things that are not important in my life.

I do not want to write about things that will not help me with my recovery.

I do not want to write about doubt and negativity.

I do not want to write about happy things.

I do not want to write.

Nicole R.

# But I Wrote About It Anyway

I don't want to write about how different this is going to be.

I don't know how strong I'll have to be to kick drugs and booze.

I don't want to write about having a sober New Years Eve

And not smoking when I want to play in the snow.

I don't want to write about how my good intentions might be lost.

I don't want to write that maybe I might not have what it takes to be successful at this.

I don't want to write about how hard it is to fill this page,

How this page is empty except for the words on it,

How this page could look like any other,

How this page is now.

It seems impossible to fill.

Perhaps it is better to leave it blank than to fake important sentences,

Sentences that are far from the truth.

Those sentences are best not written.


Angela T.

# The City

Stars and city lights twinkle out a cryptic morse code
Signalling to heaven
Its instability
And all we can say
Faced with the intangibility of this kind of distress
Is 'how beautiful'
And stare dumbfounded by our unease
Thinking privately that we feel worried
And then wake up at 2 o'clock the next morning
And can't get back to sleep

Sarah A.

# ADVICE

# Strap These Shoes

I want to write about—
Well, not just write
But devour—these words and what I am thinking.
Please don't be scared,
It's just salt in the wound.
Follow me,
I have sugar instead.

I know how it goes,
One day it's yes, another it's no,
Going in circles,
It's so hard.

To bad there's no map to follow
To lead us to sanity.
If we plant our flowers and they bloom,
Maybe we will too,
Maybe even our souls, our joy or our minds.
Then it's time, time for you to ask,
Well, hell, it's time to wake up,
Time to see the mess you made of this precious life,
The torture to your body.

Look to the sky,
Don't look down,
Just walk on,
You're better than that.

Life is a mystery that can take you far, far away
On a journey you will never forget.
I won't say it will hurt, but damn girl, it will be difficult,
So strap on those shoes and be ready to fight.
Fight your demons.
Come on now,
We've forgotten how to walk,
Like a baby on all fours.

Now we start over,
All over again,
Without the crutch we think we need.
Learn to walk with your head up.
Look to the sky,
Don't look down,
Just walk on,
You're better than that.

Life is a mystery that can take you far, far away,
On a journey you will never forget.
If you've got something to say,
Dammit girl, shout it to the world until they understand your pain!
You are a part of this world too.
Don't let anyone take that away from you.
Scream it loud!
Get rid of the hurt.
I know.

Alessandra B.

# PAIN

# *Finding Me*

I have been lost for so long
In a shroud of despair and unhappiness.
Sadness, guilt, shame, anger, resentment,
Hopelessness and unworthiness form my being.
I am unable to feel love or to give love.
Only darkness prevails.

What is it like to love yourself,
To love others, to be happy,
To have inner peace?
I do not know.

What is it like to have that maternal bond with your newborn babies,
To want to hold them, cuddle them and love them?
I do not know.
How could a mother feel repulsed by hugging, kissing
Or saying I love you to their own child?
Where did I go wrong?
Why can't I love?
I do not know.
Five deserving children were robbed of tender loving care and nurturing
Because I did not know how to love.
How humiliating
To have to be taught how to love through counselling.
I had to fake it until I made it,
And still I find it difficult or unnatural at times.
The guilt and shame of the emotional neglect I imposed on my children
is unbearable.

I was satiated with resentment and anger,
Realizing that my childhood was empty of love, hugs, kisses,
Positive emotion, encouragement and parental interest in my successes.
I only remember being yelled at,
Not being good enough,
Feeling unworthy, empty and unhappy.
No wonder I put on a brave, confident face,
But cower with fear and inferiority on the inside.
No wonder I could not love my children.
My parents did not know how to love me.

It is very hard to live a lie.
The conflict between the real me and my outer facade caught up to me.
All the negative thoughts and feelings mushroomed into depression,
Then a vicious cycle of despair, self-hatred, and emotional eating
Spiralled out of control, into alcoholism.

Now long into sobriety, my emotional hell is worse than ever.
I am just a dry drunk.
What do I do now?
Where do I go from here?
How do I heal the broken person that I am?
Will I ever know love, happiness and inner peace?

God, please help me to find me.

Sheryl M.

# Homecoming

Time, the hands on the clock ticking away.
Waiting, waiting, waiting, or whizzing by like a train.
Catch that train, I want to be on it, I want to be in it,
I don't want to miss out!
Maybe it's too fast.
Wait,
Was that my stop?
Hope I didn't miss it.
Don't want to get off.
Too much happening, too much excitement.

Anonymous

# Here Again

I remember when life was so weird and cold,
My energy level made me feel very old.
I remember when my smiles came easily,
Now I feel they come filled with questions.
I remember when the days were filled with laughter and routine,
Now I'm not sure when I will go home or have a sense of clean.

I remember when the kids were small
And every day was easy,
No drinks or drugs.
I remember when I used to look in the mirror.
Now to brush my teeth and comb my hair
Seems like a lot to bear.

I remember when God made sense and his closeness was near.
Now I need him, oh so dear.
I remember when my laughter was genuine,
And I stood tall.
Today I hope God will hear my call.

I remember when to be old was a fear.
Now I hope I make it to next year.

I remember when to eat a meal was no big deal.
Now in my home, drugs and alcohol make that unreal.

I remember when to feel was such a fear,
But to mask it brought me here.

Margaret M.

# Walking Out

Fear is a big part of my life.

There are many people, places and things in my life that I fear.

Walking out the door and back into the world after this class brings me fear.

I fear not knowing what to do or where to go,

How to act and what others will think of me.

I fear not being able to say no to my drug of choice,

To my friends,

But most of all to myself.

I fear not being accepted.

I fear I may fail as I have time and time again.

Fear is what makes me so afraid.

What is it that I truly fear?

Not knowing what will happen next?

What tomorrow will bring?

Will I be able to stay clean?

Will I ever be accepted for me?

Just me?

I fear myself,

The choices I have made,

The choices still to come.

I fear losing everything,

Like so many times before.

Lindsay S.

# Resentments

And the rain just kept pouring down.
The drizzle and grey matched my insides
And I wished I could let my tears fall
As freely as the drops from the sky,
So the sadness I felt might pour from me
And leave me clean and pure.
I wanted to open up and
Unblock all that kept me trapped.

I remembered when my kids were young.
When they were hurt, they would burst into tears
And when they were spent, it was over.
The tears would dry and they were healed.
Out would come the sun again
And they would smile and forget
Why they were sad.
They'd be on to the next thing,
The next discovery and it would be over.
I could soothe them with a few kind words of comfort
And all was well.
They didn't recall or think about it anymore
And they were open and free
And alive and happy in no time,
As if a dripping faucet had been shut off
And problems ran down the drain
And out of sight and all was forgiven.

It is the constant refrain of past hurts
Or unkind words
That blocks the sunshine
And keeps the soul in the cold, relentless, dripping rain.

Judy L.

# Cry

I told her I would call,
But instead, I wait for tears.
I wait for something to break,
For me to break.
The tears do not come.
I miss them today.
I miss the body shaking sobs today.

Please, I ask of you,
I need you.
Shake me to my core,
Make me feel,
Give me release.

Please, I beg you.
I beg for tears,
I beg.

But those tears do not come.
They are trapped
Somewhere deep inside.
Why can I not do the simple things?
Cry,
Cry and feel.

Justine N.

# My Anxiety

It lives, it breathes, it grows.
It consumes me like fire.
It's always there,
Waiting to pounce.
Whenever I think I'm OK,
It grips my brain like a vice.
I can't think.
I am paralyzed with fear.
I can't move.
There are no words,
Just a panicky emptiness.
What do I do?
What do I say?
Motionless.
Mute,
Unable to express the feeling that lies within.
Sometimes mute,
Sometimes screaming to be let out,
But always contained
Like a fire in a furnace,
Don't let it out!
It will consume all of me,
Then everything else,
So in it stays,
Consuming me instead from the inside out.
Burning, stifling, silencing, choking, suffocating,
Until I can't stand it.
I can't speak.

I can't breathe any longer.
The smoke gets in my eyes,
It is stinging, blinding,
Making grimy tears flow,
Soot and smoke.
I can't see.
It smells bad.
All the peace and beauty is gone from the world.
My throat is thick,
I can't breathe, can't swallow, can't speak,
Hands gripping my insides,
Squeezing, churning, gasping.

Chris B.

# *Broken*

Broken hearts?
Compassion, more meaning.
Broken relationship?
Disease spreads, hopeless,
Can't move forward, frozen in time.
Soul is taken.
Slowly it breaks apart,
Left to pick up the pieces.

Life.
Complicated enough, too much attraction,
Too much curiosity,
Down that same path, in that same hole.
Make up with the bottle,
Wake up, then break up,
A never ending cycle.
Drown sorrows, suffocate pain,
The bottle empties,
A stranger is revealed.
Lost grip of time.

Broken relationships, broken hearts.
Underlying control?
Lifeless.
Internal abuse, permitted,
Forgotten insults, thrown in the past,
Crave more, beg to be broken.

Why love it so?
Phenomenal obsession,
Impossible to break free,
Helpless when apart.
Lips touch with disgust,
Regret.
Freedom unseen.
Left, undone,
Empty.

What do I confide in now?

Anonymous

# Keep the Promise

To me it sounds as if all you care about is my drinking.
You wait until you know I have crossed the line
And then you attack.
Why is it so difficult for you to validate my feelings?
There is turmoil in my psyche.
You have been there.
You have seen my pain
And yet you find it easier to ignore what I say
And blame only the drink.
I feel invisible most of the time,
But when I drink you see me.
You are there, ready to say mean and hurtful things.
You have to be cruel to be kind.
I can't understand.
Help me, and not only with alcohol
But all that has made me weak and vulnerable.
Protect me as you promised many years ago.
"Your" values—as in, if I don't talk about it, it is not happening—
are wrong.
Everyone needs to be heard.
Please, I beg for me and others, to listen
And you too will learn
And we can continue our journey together.

Lynne

# Lynne . . .
## March 20th 1958

It is with a great sense of relief that the family of Lynne celebrate her death. Left to finally live a normal life are her spouse and children and granddaughters. Lynne led a life of a worthless alcoholic. Her selfishness will never be forgotten by the many family members she affected. Lynne was best known for her tireless manipulation of all who came into contact with her. She spent a lifetime as a self-serving, worthless waste of space. Lynne has proven over many years she had zero compassion for anyone other than herself. Lucky people gone before her include her father, who regretted having more children within months of her birth; her mother, who understood her daughter was a needy, ungrateful person from a very young age; her in-laws who knew what a grave mistake their only son was making when he married Lynne. This selfless angel can now go on and possibly have the life he always deserved. Her children and their spouses will now be able to have peace from all the pain of an uncaring alcoholic mother and the shame she caused them. Her granddaughters will be blessed with only knowing they had a G.G. We thank God every day they are young enough to forget. A celebration of Lynne's death will take place every day from this day forward. In lieu of flowers, please hug your children and thank God she is gone. Her sisters and brothers pray that her soul be sent to hell for the unforgiving pain and shame she has caused them. May she not rest but remain in the devil's home where she belongs. The world is a better place.

I wrote this after my husband told me he had written my obit. I had a need to make sure it was written correctly.

Lynne

# *Stop*

Stop, Daddy, stop—don't yell at them.
Please, Daddy, please beat on me.

Stop, Daddy, stop pushing me so hard.
Please, Mommy, please rescue me—it's a start.

Stop, Daddy, stop—don't love me more.
Please, Alli, please don't hate, I implore.

Stop, Karen, stop—you don't need anymore.
Please, Karen, please keep feeding me.

Stuff, Karen, stuff—don't let them see.
Smile, Karen, smile—entertain me.

Love, Karen, love—that's all you need.
Run, Karen, run—he'll hurt you indeed!

Cry, Karen, cry—you must let it go.
Try, Karen, try—though it's all you know.

Fly, Karen, fly—you can heal your heart.
Stop, Karen, stop—it's about to start.

Goodbye Pain.

Karen E.

# Rearranged

Someone's rearranged the furniture.
Everyone knows that would drive me insane.
Everything is in its place,
Perfect order,
Perfect placement,
Perfect flow,
It must be Perfect!

You know, I've always been like this.
It drove my mother nuts, my sister would mess things up on purpose,
and Dad,
Well, Daddy thought I was magnificent.

Someone rearranged the furniture.
Everything is in its place.
The pictures are hung wrong,
The baskets are in disarray.
Everyone knows it drives me insane.

I must keep it neat and tidy, then no one sees the mess,
The messy emotions inside me,
The disorder in my head.
They know this drives me crazy.
Perfect order is what I crave.

Someone rearranged the furniture.
How dare they be so bad!
For order is the only thing I can truly hold.

Brown and purple don't go together, it looks like a bruise,
Resembling my broken heart.
My mind I'm going to lose.

Someone rearranged the furniture.
I know I'll go insane.
For change is so uncomfortable, it causes me so much pain.
The flowers here, the magazines there, wait, that table does not belong there!
How could they do this to me, knowing it's so very wrong?
Someone rearranged the furniture, rearranged my furniture, rearranged me.

Karen E.

# Trapped

A hollow feeling from the essence of strife,
Slanderous words spoken amidst the wind,
Upon our thoughts it will subdue all desire,
Standing on the stage,
Distraught and suffering.

Cold hands and ignorance won't compliment,
But it's okay to throw dirt on them.
They don't have feelings,
And so it remains a distant dream.
Souls tortured and trapped,
Dependent on the windows of light,
Following this numbness around this echoed cry.

Nonetheless, our actions became criminal,
And our words no more.
They scared the life right out of me,
Following my last feeling right through the door.
They smiled and shook my hand,
Angry and powerless.

So we prepare to paint over the landscape,
For it is now covered with holes.
It loses life for every star.
Once they grow old,
Each one has been corrupted.
Each one thrown amongst the rest of the loathing,
Each one has fallen,
Spread into a background of emptiness.

Alessandra B.

# Day Two: Home

I'm not sure I'll stay here.
I do have a place to go.
It's called home, and this isn't it.
This is a hell of an inhumane place,
With nothing to do. But I have somewhere to go.

Lynne M.

# No Encore

I tumble along,
Clumsy and noticeable.
I am no longer graceful
And elegant in my disguise.
I could no longer mute it,
Stifle the cries
For the unwanted assistance.

I aim to please,
Now missing the target completely,
Too clouded and foggy to fully see,
My vision is not what it once was.

The character has changed completely
In this poorly written story,
Or my portrayal is not up to par.
Bad acting, I suppose,
I am now exposed.

Sheena S.

# Alone

A vast empty space,
A deep dark place,
A hollow hole inside,
I cannot climb out.
Even the single tear sliding down my cheek is lonely,
Having no others to follow it.
I've been there,
I've been so frighteningly alone.
Desperate for happiness,
Desperate for companionship,
Loneliness is misery,
Loneliness is despair.
Drowning in my own sorrows,
I am not a strong swimmer.

Crying myself into a deep slumber,
Where even my dreams are sad,
It's that feeling in the pit of your stomach,
The craving for warmth.
It's being in a crowded room filled with loud chatter
And still feeling utterly alone.
Wanting to curl up into a ball and let the tears fall,
But they won't.

It's standing alone on a balcony,
Feeling the cold night breeze,
Staring at the full moon,
Wondering if it's as lonely as you.

It's watching the sun go down
And pondering if it is sad to go,
Or am I just sad to see it go?
Empty laughs,
Fake smiles,
Honest signs,
Whispers,
That don't seem to change a thing.
Everyone dies alone.

Sheena S.

# Depression

Depression is the blackness within.

Depression takes root.

Depression spreads like a weed.

Depression flourishes.

Depression is the dark night.

Depression allows no light to penetrate the surface.

Depression suffocates.

Depression kills.

Depression is death.

Anonymous

# Spaces

Fear of lonely spaces in between,
What do you have hiding in the seam?
Don't look now, freeze that face,
Wondering where you go from this place,
Past stories that were dark inside,
Death.

Sits closer, so still,
You whisper to your friend,
Did you write your last will?
Leaving now to face it alone,
You don't think they're going home.
Flashbacks are winning the race.
Just a moment, don't try to twist fate.

Fear and wishing it was in a book,
Just a chapter on life,
How sweet it would be.
Bright lights, close your eyes,
Stepping back in the shadows that embrace,
Trying to find something you haven't erased.
A piece of faith is what you need,
Why hold a picture of the key?

Pauline W.

# They

Between the shadows,
Disguised as hope,
Waiting for the children,
To attack their innocence,
It's where emptiness slowly creeps,
Behind the smiles and the winks.

The working androids
Trample me down
Inside my mind,
Where my fear pretends to sleep.

Messed up,
But I'll keep standing,
Even though there's not much headroom.
When I'm like this, I can't cry,
I don't want the world to know.

They begin to destroy for now.
Just curl up under this cloud of gloom,
It just hurts too much,
Alone in my room.

I want to tell you about this dream I had,
It was so fine.

Happiness was in the palm of my hand,
Hope was there too,
Dancing like grass in the sky.

So pretty, calmness came through a gentle breeze.
I felt like I was back in time,
Simple, yet dumbfounded until I awoke,
I felt so used.
I couldn't figure out why.

But I realized that someone had closed my fist,
Each finger to the bone,
It fell to the earth as sand.

Each bit of self-control,
Just the thoughts and the cravings won't go,
Just what I feared,
Until this day.

I'm not understanding this black and white.
People still lie,
People still hate,
It eats me up inside,
Because I fear it won't ever end.

Some days I feel like laughing.
The glimmer in my eye
Decides to come back again,
It takes a chance, but I cannot.

Because I know why,
I know why they lied.
So my mind finds ways to escape,
Ways to sleep and dream.

Those who lie in the dirt,
Waiting for the sunlight on their faces,
While we hide in our caves of addiction,
Away from the light, hiding,
Becoming shadows of hate.

Through this world of grey,
I just can't figure out why,
Although I have figured out their game,
Why they all lied,
Why they pretend
That our soul will never die,
When they really know the truth.

In the end we are so damaged,
It eventually fades away
When you corrupt your body.

Your life is so meaningless,
So I might as well cry,
Because they want us to.

Alessandra B.

# Somewhere and Nowhere

I don't even know, with nowhere to go,
But there is always somewhere to go,
And we must have come from somewhere.
From where? I don't really care.
I got lost one day—I went astray,
And regret it to this very day.
I wonder why it is so,
I hope to never really know.
I don't want to know anyway,
That way it will be OK.
It is a simple future
But a troubled past.
I am sure it will not last.

Nowhere to go, nothing to say,
I wander idly around the bay,
Hoping for the sun to shine one ray.
I'm not feeling very well today.

Lynne M.

# A Real Christmas

I want to write about Christmas,
How it's supposed to be this great time
And everyone is happy
Without a care in the world.
You see these communities where everyone is buying gifts for everyone,
Without a care in the world.
People should think of the real meaning of Christmas:
The homeless people out there,
The people who are on social assistance,
The people who don't have jobs—
What are they going to tell their kids when there is nothing under the tree?

Anonymous

# Letting Go

Letting go of all the guilt and shame.

Letting go of all my past bullshit.

Letting go of the fear inside me that is sometimes so unbearable.

Letting go of all these thoughts of ending my life.

Letting go of self harm,

Self-sabotage,

Self-destruction.

Letting go of all this hurt and pain I have caused.

Letting go is hard for me,

I feel as if I am the only one,

I feel alone.

Letting go sucks.

Letting go of old ideas,

Letting go of all this shit,

Letting go.

Shelley H.

# No Connection

Look out the window at the lights flashing by,
Hear the click-clack,
Feel the rumble,
Pink Floyd sounding through my ear buds,
But I have to get off.
Have to slow down,
Have to focus,
Take a walk instead.

Tick, tick,
Click-clack.
The train slows down.
I hear the conductor call,
Is he talking to me?
I'm the only one getting off,
How odd.
Where is everybody?

It's quiet out here, it's very dark.
Where should I go?
Which way is home?
I need some directions.
Where is the peace and support on this damn Google map?

I think I'm in a dead zone—no connection.
Will I get where I need to go?

I see something in the distance,
A lit window.
I wonder if that house is a home,
I wonder if they have a dog.

Jacquie B.

# Hush, Little One

I find the silence very hard.
The sound of silence echoes in my head
like a freight train at full speed.
I'm just a child in a silent world called home.
Quiet, little one, no one wants to hear you.
My little head yearns for a familiar sound.
Echo, echo, echo, is all I hear.
My young mind is eager to learn and listen.
Music, what is music?
Instruments, what are they?
Sorry, little one, no sound for you.
Hey sister . . . let's talk.
Twins, you know, have their own language.
Oh wow the silence is finally broken!
Then I hear, "Hush little ones . . . Daddy is near.
It's not safe to make sounds, so quiet, little ones . . . hush."
Oh my . . .
Back to the deafening silence once again.
Yearning to be heard is just a wish
and everyone knows wishes
don't always come true.
Silence, little ones, hush.

Esther B.

# To Remember Me

I remember when it didn't hurt so much.
I can't remember the lights
But I know the pain.
I remember when love was routine.
But I didn't catch it.
I remember when I was small,
But sadly, I am still small.

I remember when it became a time not to remember,
When I thought I still heard and felt him out of a pretty little bottle.
I remember when it was okay to stand tall,
When I thought peace of mind still mattered.
Maybe to remember is going to make me better.
But, I must remember what to forget.

Shauna W.

# The Walking Dead

They brought gifts and flowers,
Smiles were few,
Spoke meaningless words over hours,
Expressions so untrue.

As my world eased on,
The night faded away,
Rested in darkness,
I was reluctant to believe,
Yet longing for truth.

Irony is what I thought,
They are already dead and gone,
But from whose clock does time vanish and rot?
I cannot move on.

Scars hide the pain in reality,
I knew not what I saw.
I cried myself to sleep,
The world has ignored your fatal flaw.

Alessandra B.

# The New Kid

I remember being the new kid,
Standing in the hall
With my mom, my brother, and the principal.
A knock on the door,
A harried teacher,
Busy sounds inside,
A quick introduction.

Bye, Mom.
Fighting back tears,
I have to be strong,
I have to look brave.
No tears.
Look as if you do this every year.
You do.
Stand at the front,
Smile wide when the teacher says your name,
Look out over the sea of strange faces.

Walk down the aisle.
Don't pass out.
Don't throw up.
Just sit down,
Take a breath.
Pretend you're busy checking out your new stuff.
Don't look up,
Don't catch anyone's eye,
Just look ahead.

Someone hands out the paper.
Write your name at the top,
Answer the questions.
Don't look up.
Don't catch anyone's eye.
Whatever you do, don't put up your hand.
Just do your work.
Pray that recess never comes.

Chris B.

# I Don't Do Returns

I fumble with my words
When I used to speak so eloquently.
I struggle with my thoughts
When I used to think so clearly.
I used to turn so many heads
And see the smiling faces.
Now they bow in shame,
Not knowing how to take this.
I used to carry on such interesting conversations with ease,
No reservations,
So animated and entertaining,
Full of life,
Like a dance.
Now this dimming light bulb
Doesn't stand a chance.

Sheena S.

# Not a Love Letter

I am determined to fight for my survival.

I almost killed my mother when I was born.

I was over two months early,

She hemorrhaged so much she nearly died.

I think she's resented me to this day

For the physical ramifications and distress my birth caused her.

I know I've always resented her.

I died in my childhood from lack of love,

Then quite nearly died a few times in my twenties.

I just went a little too far.

But as usual, I proved to be a survivor.

The doctors say I should have been dead fifteen years ago,

But that just isn't happening.

I have to outlive that bitch of a mother.

And it's fun to survive.

I came to this place as another way to survive.

The fight never ends and neither does the fight that lives inside of me.

I will keep going no matter what.

As for my mother,

I haven't spoken with her in quite some time.

Lynne M.

# *Hands of Fate*

People say they care,
But they don't.
I'm just a rock on the road,
Step on me anytime.
Yes, I'm in the hands of fate,
It's my friend.
My eating disorder, Edie Edie,
Will be with me until I become a consecrated angel.
People say they care,
But they don't.
Edie, get me there soon.

Laura Y.

# ADVICE

# Friendship

Friend, it's always nice to think of you
And the good times that we share,
And of how grand it's always been,
To have an angel who cares.

Laura Y.

# Stand With Me

You finally stared back at me and understood everything. I've waited for this. We are too much alike for this not to have happened. It has been lonely these years after I chose this path and you continued on the one I couldn't maintain anymore. I was too tired. Drained. You had more in you. I let go. Walked away and sometimes it felt like you had turned your back on me. But if you had turned around and looked at me you would have seen yourself in my mirror. And I know that you could not look at yourself that way.

I've waited. Kept my distance. Wondering when you would see what I have known all along. I tell stories of those days and our names are interchangeable. It could have been either of us. It caught up to me first. I couldn't stand on my own two feet. You used to hold me up, hold us up. But the weight was too much and I couldn't stand anymore. I fell and now have found a way to stand on my own again. You have fallen too. Please stand with me again. I have missed you.

Justine N.

# Peace

It takes time, love and support to find peace in yourself.
The love, only you can give yourself.
Support you gather from your loved ones.
Only then can you truly find the inner peace that your soul desires.

Anonymous

# STRUGGLE

# A Sober Life

I want to write about my experience at detox.
I came in and don't recall what day or time I arrived.

I must be really sick with this disease.

Why do I have it?
Why can't I stop drinking?

Before I came here to Womankind, I was out for six and a half days straight.
I only have a brief recollection of what happened to me.

I totally blacked out for long periods in the day and night.
I do remember trying not to lose my keys, my cigarettes and my bankcard.
I have lost them many times when I've been out.

As of today, I have been sober for a day and a half.
The joy is lifting and some moments are coming back.
I feel ashamed of all of them.

I am really glad to be alive this time, and coming back.
But now I have to face all the people that I trust, especially my children.
They don't deserve that.
I feel really badly that I didn't show up for them on the weekends,
I didn't sober up.
All I remember is an argument with their father saying I couldn't see them anymore.
He was sick and tired of me popping in and out of their lives.

Why am I such a failure as a mom?
Why do I always let them down?

I need help to stop drinking.
I am here to get that help.

Help me live a sober life.

Leah W.

# Being Poor

So you keep looking and looking
and thinking
whats the difference between
me and them
what do they have
that I don't
and you figure
someone must have loved them more
or God loves them more
or they just decided to love themselves more
but what ever it is
it signifies a lack in you that makes you bitter
and withdrawn
you figure you don't even know how to deserve
what they've been given
that instinctual worthiness
that completeness
that intimate understanding of safety and courage and trust that closes
the circle
how can you stand beside that
and not want to shrink
and not want to beat your children
when you come home from working two jobs
to despise the sight of every shabby possession
threatened by dirty little fingers
that seem to ask
am I enough
to account

for your present
your past
what can you divine about your future
based on this couch cushion
and wonder how to survive
every insulting hour
of being less than

if stress is a tension of opposites
then I am torn between
the faint possibility
hope offers
and the overwhelmingly evident reality of destitution and despair
I navigate through in the courtyards of government housing projects

I can feel the crowding anxious sadness
of a grown man
trying to crawl back into a dream of youth
but being jolted into reality by graceless spasms of pain
but he prays
he prays

Sarah A.

# Fearless Forever

Fear is a cold word, thought and feeling.
I fear my life,
I fear for my kids,
I fear losing myself.
Fear or fearless,
Both I feel, but fear more,
I hate being in fear.

Scared, fearful,
Not only because it's scary
But because it's there,
Fear of not being loved,
Fear of being loved,
Fear.

I hate fear.
Fear creates addicts,
And I'm one of them.
Fear of me,
I don't know who I am,
Fear I'll never find me,
Fear I'll die.

Fear is a strong word.
I'm in fear now,
Fear that I won't be good enough.
I wish fear did not exist.
Fear of society,

Fear of no control,
Fear of finding who I am.
What if I'm nothing?
I fear that.

I hate life as it stands.
I always thought I was fearless.
Fear is such a strong word,
I'm not strong overall.

Fearing me is fearing you,
Fearless is what I want to be.
Forever.
Fearless.

Kandi S.

# Gift to Self

Don't step on my shoes, don't stomp on my heart.
I might break or I might just cry.
Please spin me around, my worlds collide.
But for all those reasons, I could not fly.
Give me more, the addition calls.
My head is spinning, eyes are burning,
Every street corner
Looking for a familiar face,
But all I see is the devil.
My hands are shaking,
My knees will give out,
My heart's beating fast.
What do I do?
It's all coming so quickly.
But I need it.
No, *you* want it.
Get out of my head.
Inside and out it hurts so bad,
I wish I could just go back
To when I didn't know of all this evil,
To a time where things were much simpler than this.
Take me there, I cry out.

And just as I go to walk through the door
Someone holds my hand.
And another hand,
We connect to each other.
All my guardians from up above,

Loved ones who have moved on to the spirit world,

Holding my hands tightly away from the hurt and pain and suffering.

They are saving my life one heartbeat at a time.

The drugs are pulling me one way,

And the spirits have it torn between us.

I take their hands as I stroll towards them.

You are worth more than this, they say,

You have a life to live,

So go out and live it.

But always remember, we will be by your side.

When you're about to fall,

Trust us and you will find your path,

Believe and you can, you will, conquer this demon.

And then they were gone.

I had a choice to make,

Which wolf to feed,

But I already knew in my heart,

I will feed the wolf inside of me.

A gift to self.

Alessandra B.

# Getting What We Want

I cannot bring myself to put down the coffee today
I'm trying to get to sometime in the future
where everything is done
and taken care of

where all the fruits of my labour and patience
wait
to fill me up with their promise

what is promise after all
the marrow of expectation
its content is the same
only now
it's yours

but like most domesticated things
it often comes coerced
and beyond the fleeting thrill of recognition
comes a more concerting sense of obligation
and guilt
perhaps some disappointment . . .
the source of which is hard to locate
whether it emanates from the conquered
or the conqueror
or even more intangibly the conquering

Sarah A.

# My Thoughts

My thoughts are hard to express,
So I push you on to read the rest.
Sometimes I want to end it all,
But then I make a simple call.
I call my mom, my guiding light,
She tells me that I have to fight,
And everything will be all right.
I once was lost in drugs and booze,
But now I have too much to lose.
All I have left is positive thinking,
Or else my hopes will end up sinking.
So all of you who wish me luck,
Really, baby, I don't give a fuck.
'Cause luck is not what I really need,
'Cause strong is what I have to be.

Sonya T.

# The Origin of Abandonment Issues

That's all you have to do, just be alive.
Don't have to be grateful—
Who would be grateful to be a survivor?
Just be alive,
Relax girl,
And take the cheque,
Take the diagnosis,
Take the housing,
Take the treatment,
Take the Christmas alone.
Because happy families are all a lie.
Anyhow, my life is anti-climactic now.
Anything after he was found guilty is my life.
My life is ontological insecurity
And I feel as if there is no family,
No peers,
No career,
No pets . . .
No identity.
Which 12 step fellowship do I fit into?
I don't know. I am still the same little girl who said,
"The Emperor has no clothes."
And I pay the price, everyday, for pointing that out.
Who said that being a pioneer
In the women's movement was easy?
All I had to do was go to court and say the truth.
And I get stuck with this dilemma
Of not belonging anywhere.

All I had to do was to not accept the violence.

I became somebody's hero . . .

Somewhere . . .

Someplace.

Maybe I am a hero on the bus

When the hijab-wearing lady smiles with me

While my tattoos show on my Mormon arms.

Maybe I am a hero to my lover who savors my passion.

Well, maybe somebody, somewhere

Will see my courage.

Some day.

And maybe I will find peace with my place in the world.

April A.

# Fear Knocked at my Door

I opened the door.
Oh my gosh, it was my crazy mixed up
"Fucked up in different words."
My life had become so unmanageable
I couldn't even sleep at night.
Toss and turn, up and down,
Sleep, awake,
That's all I do.
Fear—what does fear mean to me?
It means not having to be an addict anymore,
By facing the fear dead on.
Man oh man, does this ever scare the shit out of me.
It terrifies me when I really think about it.
I know what I have to do
And I'm attacking it full force.
Because it is so important,
I'm doing it for my family.
It's so scary!
Fear of failing.
Fear of not being a good mom.
Fear of not being a good wife.
But I know I can do it,
So I think I'm going to take all my fear
And do a few things with it.
Face it head on, tackle the world.
Take each day one day at a time
And say goodbye to the fear.
"YOU'RE NOT ALLOWED TO RUN MY LIFE ANYMORE!"
Ciao baby!
Get out of my life, fear.
No one here no more,
That crazy lady's gone!

Karrie S.

# Pieces of Me

To me, it sounds like guilt and shame.
I hurt all over.
I have so much pain
I can't even look at myself in the mirror.
I lost all my self-respect and self-worth.
I hate myself for what I have done
To you, my only son.
I promised you I would never do it again
But I did.
I did not care at all.
All I cared about was my next high or my next fix,
NOT YOU.

I feel so guilty for letting you down.
I love you and I'm sorry.
I know I'm not worth your forgiveness.
The shame, the guilt is eating me up inside
And it hurts so bad that I want to die,
From the pain I feel for you and now your little brother.
I'm so sorry you have to say bye to mommy forever
Unless mommy says enough of this,
No more pain,
No more shame for you or your brother.
Mommy is coming back for you, my babies,
Because you guys mean the world to me and nothing else.
I will love myself so I can love another.

Sonya T.

# Doing All I Have To Do

That's all you have to do.
All you have to do is get clean, Karrie.
Come on, it's not that hard.
But the thought of being so sick to my stomach
Sickens me,
It sends the worst knots in my tummy!
But I know somehow I must tell myself,
It's okay, I've got to go away.
So on the phone I call rehab after rehab.
None will let me still take my meds
To help me through this.
But wait, there's one more place, Womankind.
The woman was so nice and kind to me on the phone
As I tell her my story,
But it was so hard to get it out,
I was high, too high. Heroin!
So I said I GTG, I'll call you tomorrow.
So I put it off for another week!
What's wrong with me?
I know what happens if I'm not clean by 12 months.
My son, TJ, I'll lose him forever.
I can't do this, I say!
All you have to do, you stupid ass,
Is get your lazy ass off the couch,
Stop thinking about your high
And get your beautiful family back!
I call myself all kinds of names, beat myself up!
Till one night I had a dream

That my son was adopted out
And I couldn't deal!
No way, I said—that's my child.
I will do what I have to do, it's not that hard.
Now I sit here at Womankind!
24 days clean.
I've never been happier
And I am on my way to getting my beautiful son back today.
That's all I have to do.
Why didn't I see it that way?
Why was I so blind, selfish and even stupid?
Now I'm clean, so relaxed and not hating my life.
I've made some new friends along the way!
Thanks for pushing me!

Karrie S.

# Haven't Been to Jail, YET

Wrestling with demons.
My addiction is the deep void within.
It is skeletons hanging on a clothes line.
Vulgar things no one likes to look at,
Or we look at and cringe,
Once again rubber necking away.
No one wants to admit to being
A dirty mistrustful addict.
What tastes so good inhaling
Tastes like crap verbally exhaling.
Why do I get a lump in my throat
Every time I identify as an addict?
It's like admitting to an affair with the devil,
And my own family disowns me
For carrying a demon seed child in my belly.
No one is looking forward to its expulsion
Into the mean streets or in the confines of home—
The baby addict born of a mother's infidelity from Christ.
Her tryst with the devil is angst for life.
Hell on earth.
Death for all.
Jail for all.
And one more visit to an institution
To maybe expel the devil's spawn into a toilet,
A cesspool deemed fit for shit,
Never a cuddly warm receiving blanket,
Always fire and brimstone.
When does the demon stop winning?
Does the bell ring to signal the end of the bout?
Does my bleeding forehead signify termination of addiction?
I pray for redemption,
One more round at Womankind.
Hope one, Devil zero.

April A.

# I Find the Silence

I want to know where it is inside of me,
And what to do with it some time.
I try to ask for help
But no one is ever there.
So I keep all my shit inside of me
And that works a lot when I do that.
Someday I will be free from it
And be free without hurt.
And I won't be mad at anyone that I hurt.
I don't want to hurt anyone.
But I hurt my boy and girl a lot.
I just wish I could get all my mad out of myself.
Some ways I can get help is by going to NA and AA,
Telling them what is going on with me,
And getting inside help.
All I want is to be clean and happy
And free from all things
That I was taking inside of me.
I don't have a lot of time
But I take it one day at a time,
For me,
And not run away from help all my life.
I have been doing that.
I don't want to do that anymore.
Mom and Dad keep telling me
That I am no good at all.
But I know I am a good woman
And have a good heart.
Sometimes I don't know where it comes from inside of me.

Jean F.

# Role Play

I am ashamed of myself
For what I have done in the past.
The past is in the past,
I cannot undo anything I've done or said.

Today there is hope,
Hope of a bright and happy future.
The future is unknown,
I can only hope.

Shame is real, I am not.
I fill my head with what I hear, what I read.
I tell myself it's real.
It's not real,
It's not how I feel.

Only positive thoughts,
Positive thoughts all the time.
Maybe it's good,
Maybe it's better to be honest with myself,
To be honest with others.

I can't fake my way through recovery,
As I fake my way through life.
You're sober now, you should be proud!
Be proud to be sober?
I feel ashamed for having such a problem in the first place.
The more accomplishments I have in life, the more ashamed I feel.

I wasted everything away—I wasted myself away.
Time spent wasted
Is time wasted.
So much time wasted.

I can't tell my father, he is so proud.
Why should he feel ashamed as I do?
I will let him believe the lie,
The lie that is me,
All I am is a lie.
Always trying to be whatever I'm supposed to be,
I'm never me.

Nicole R.

# When I Was Young

When I was young,
My first memory was of light, smiles, laughter and joy,
My parents holding me tight,
Playing outside until the wind caught up and the rain came down.
We would run, jump, and play.
Play.
I don't remember how to play anymore.
Time was of no consequence, no meaning.
I was free to be myself.
As time moved on and I grew up,
Light began to fade and the darkness seeped into my eyes.
My childlike ways were gone.

I miss those days.
No worries, as they would say.
I always said if I could, I would be four forever.
All my friends couldn't wait to get older, but not me.
I'm a kid at heart and I always will be.
Now when I look back, I can also remember the fear as a child,
The yelling and screaming across the room,
Me, crying on my bed alone.
Maybe this shaped who I am,
Although it's only part of my childhood,
But the pain of that will always linger in my heart.
My teacher once told me to never change,
But I didn't understand,
I thought change was the only constant in this world.
A whirlwind of confusion, I think I'm still lost in the dark.
I want the joy and the smiles back.
I want to learn how to play again,
Play again, like when I was young.

Alessandra B.

# Starting Fresh

And the rain just kept pouring down,
Like the waves of worry and anxiety,
Building a scaffolding of negative outcomes,
Beliefs about self.
What was happening around me?
People I knew and loved,
Their canoes drifted farther and farther away,
Until I couldn't see their faces anymore.
Could I see my face anymore?
Did I even recognize my face anymore?
What lies beneath?
Therein lies the million-dollar question.
I would think I knew,
Only to realize that the corridor in the maze I was in
Was taking me down a path I did not want to go,
Or did not understand,
Trying to climb my way back to the surface
From the deep pit of loneliness,
Only to lose my grip once I neared the top.

"Oh I once was lost" . . . and still am.
Where lie the answers?
Is the beginning within myself?
I just want to be able to have a good answer
When I meet my maker and he asks me,
"My daughter, what have you done
With the gifts that I have given you?" and
"How have you made a difference in this world?"

I am scared, lonely and uncertain.

Am I strong enough?

Am I equipped with enough skill sets

To make it in this world?

Logically I believe I am,

Based on what I have accomplished in the past.

I just want to start fresh knowing who I am this time.

Debbie

# Please Protect Me . . .
## I Want to Live

Only for a moment was I lost.
I went wherever the moment was taking me.
I am fully present in mind, body and spirit
Now that I am clean—
Like making sugar cookies,
Churning the butter and sugar to the desired consistency,
A skill honed through the years,
Confidently knowing it is right.

For a mere moment,
Do I lose my place in the world when I relapse?
Spiritually I am never lost.
I have the tools from 14 years
Of wanting, working and breathing a less than perfect program.
If I get into panic mode,
I forget about all the meetings,
Detoxes, rehabs, doctors, nurses and hospitals,
And all the 12-step calls where I was attended to.
God gives me signs along the way so I don't get lost.
My gratitude list reflects that my higher power is there for me.
When I get lost, my addiction gets replaced with co-dependency.
I look for external validation from my lover's eyes.
My lover fills that gaping empty void inside my soul.

Giving of myself, bringing comfort to others,
Helps me and others.

I strut down the street after eating at the Wesley,
I put music in my ears to block out the using addict's mantra,
"Got any spare change?"
Hence, I have no fear of dealers, side alleys or wrong turns.
I am a good person living in an imperfect world.
My higher power likes me to call, text or email.
The bill from my cell phone is always free.
Amen.

April A.

# Crossroads

There are moments in our lives when we find ourselves at a crossroads.
I have found so many crossroads in my life.

I can honestly say I never thought I would be sitting here in a treatment centre.
I knew I had a problem
But I never wanted to admit it out loud.
It was always so hush, hush.
It was like an unspoken rule.

People say I have hit rock bottom,
But what is rock bottom?
I think that it's never too late to become or do something great.
Every single human is special
And for myself to be sitting here took everything inside me,
It took everything to finally say,
Hey, I'm an addict.
Funny, huh?
It doesn't sound so bad anymore.

When I lost my two children, I stood at a crossroads.
Either I go down one road or the other.
Well I chose the best choice at the time, or so I thought,
But really, I don't feel so stuck anymore.

Is it freedom or is it that I have been coming to crossroads all my life and I'm tired?
Fuck it, I'm tired.

Crystal R.

# Not This Time

Wrestling with demons that are inside of me,
My addiction trying,
Trying to take over, it is easy to see
That this struggle I will face every day.
I go down on my knees.
God, don't let this take over, I need to stay.
I've done this once, I've done it before.
I've been told I'm so much better,
I'm worth so much more.
These drugs are not going to win,
Not this time.
I'll get through this, I'll kick its behind.
Why was it so easy, and now it's so rough.
I don't get it, but I can do it.
I know it, I'm tough.
I'll deal with my pain, I'll deal.
I'll deal with my hurt.
I can finally stop wearing little mini-skirts.
I'm sitting here with nothing left to lose
Except for a decision,
What path do I choose?

Dana D.

# I Always Wanted To

I always wanted to
But I didn't have a fighting chance.
I was born.
I always wanted to
I can't walk.
I always wanted to
Grow up normal.
I always wanted to . . .

No, no, no.
I don't want to,
Don't hit me again,
I don't want to
Let you see me cry.
I don't want to
Grow up and maybe die.
I don't want to
Be around as you kick me down to die.

I want to marry my prince charming,
I want to have a family.
Oh, how I cry.

I want to drink a little more,
So I don't have to sit and cry.
No, no,
Please don't walk out the door.
I always wanted to make this marriage work,
I don't want to take this drug of mine.

I don't want to
Be alive each day.
I sit down and cry.
Leave me alone to my own demise.

Wait, wait, I have a reason to be here
Wanting my beautiful, healthy children of mine
To have me alive, and healthy to love.
Yes, yes,
I always wanted to have a chance at life.

So here I am, learning how to cry,
Without the drug of mine.
Smile, laugh, be giddy, you see,
I always wanted to,
Because it's all about me,
If I want it to be.

How much can I take?
I see a different woman in the make.
It's all about me, for goodness sake!

Goodbye, Goodbye, Goodbye.

Ligia D.

# Turning the Clock

Personally, I don't fit into any category.

How incorrect this statement is!

I'm an alcoholic,

A recovering alcoholic, that is!

I have allowed this demon, which I call poison, to strip me of my dignity.

It has cost me many things in my life that I value very much.

The respect of my children, money, job, legal issues, just to name a few.

When I was experiencing pain and unhappiness,

I turned to this demon for relief.

It wasn't better, just worse.

The poison had consumed me.

All I want is inner peace and self worth again.

I just have to take it one day at a time.

If I could only turn back time.


Brenda L.

# *How I Feel*

I'm here to stay. Or I could choose to go.
I have nowhere to go.
I feel trapped.
I feel alone, sad.
I feel like crying.
I need support.
I want someone to be here,
Like I'm there for them.
Why can't they come?
I want to see them.
Why does this bother me so much?
Shit, it sucks.

I'm tired of giving so much.
I'm so selfish!
I never worried before.
That's not true,
I really do care.

You do, you need this.
You need this so badly,
You can taste it.
I can't keep doing this,
I'm going nowhere fast.
Keep my head high, I'm worth it.
Keep it together.
I'm strong.

I am sad.
I feel like crying all the time.
Happy, sad, happy, sad.
What is it?
Who knows?
Keep clean.
I need a smoke!
Quit it.
I feel like dirt.
Why are you so down?
I want to feel happy.
It never lasts long.
I'm so emotional.
Such a crybaby.
Suck it up!

I feel pain, real pain, don't like it.
I'm thirsty.
I need a drink.
Wait!
That's all I do, Man.
I need some patience.
Can I get patience?
Where can I get it?
Can I buy it somewhere?

I love people, sometimes.
Just keep going,
I'll get there someday,
Easy does it.
I care if I stay clean.
I know you care.
Why wouldn't you?

Elaine W.

# ADVICE

# *Grow*

Each day we add to all we know,
As the time goes by, we learn to grow.
Beginning with some baby steps,
Love, forgive, heal and accept.
So start again from seed so slow,
Be patient, sisters, we will grow.

Karon B.

# Today is the Day

It's the day of today.
The world was once bold,
Now in these times, garbage fills our minds,
It fills our homes
And parks where our children play
And where our dogs bark.
If we go on these ways,
Each and every day,
Our earth will be no more.
So before we pollute,
Think of our children.
Please take care of our parks today.

Laura Y.

# *Morning*

I wake and breathe the morning air. It is misty. Full of damp dog and wet leaves. The downy comforter wraps my sweaty body. My hand flops and pumps, trying to hit the off button on the radio.

A thousand ways to make me smile he whispers, tempting me with his deep voice. He sounds like CBC and coffee. I stretch and groan. Flex like a cat before I tumble out and pad on thick carpet to the kitchen and the espresso machine.

My neighbours move like shadows behind layers of sheer curtains. My mind is on the paper nestled up against the front door. More dead in Japan. Taxes rising. Promises broken.

I let the dogs out to pee. Drizzling rain from heaven spanks the leaves of my Catulpa tree and the dripping pocks the canvas cover of the hot tub.

There are no tomorrows. Only today. I lift the coffee to my lips. The scalding liquid burns my tongue and I gasp. The scent is better than the bitter taste, the sharp burn. My big toe twitches with shades of arthritis and I forget the day's plan. Is it early Alzheimer's I wonder or simply the oozing out of details from the gray sponge inside my head?

I pick up my pen and write. It is a day of being. I hold it gently and tease out the words that need to come.

Gail M.

# RELATIONSHIPS

# Ice Cream and Needles

Nervous coffee dates,
Uncertainty,
Feeling loved, feeling wanted,
Needing someone,
Moving in for the first time; just a boy and me, ugly me.

He wanted to be there.
Eyes like seawater, hair like wheat,
He wanted to be there.

Pills.
Dragging the mattress onto the living room floor.
Warmth, glowing warmth, and creeping sickness.
Buckets of chocolate ice cream and kisses.
Falling asleep surrounded by ashtrays,
Empty ice cream cartons, underwear and needles.

He wanted to be there.
Eyes like seawater, hair like wheat,
He wanted to be there.

Fighting.
No money.
He always spent the money.
His seawater eyes glistening,
Beautiful.
It was slipping through my fingers, like sand—the colour of his hair.

He wanted to be there.
Eyes like seawater, hair like wheat,
He wanted to be there.

More fighting, more pills,
Moving out.
It's my fault.
It's his fault.
I never wanted it to get so bad.
I never thought I would get so bad.

Now we talk from treatment centres,
Cry, apologize and proclaim our love,
But it can never happen again.

Suzanne C.

# On the Other Side of You

I've found acceptance for your betrayals
Still doesn't mean I want to see you
It means I understand a little more now
And have stopped blaming you for everything
I see I didn't make things easy
Being together took a lot out of both of us
I don't know why we endured so long
Maybe that answer will come in time too
Thank you for helping me through
Because for as much as we destroyed each other
We were there to care and protect too
I don't know if I would have survived
Maybe I would have survived better
Like I've grown since we've been apart
Or maybe I would have been taken to darker places
I will never know
Because what's passed has passed
And all we have is now
I thank you for helping me grow stronger
In your messed up twisted kind of way
The struggles and pains you put me through
Have made me who I am today
I love me and couldn't be happier
With the life that was waiting for me
On the other side of you

Andrea E.

# (sorry)

Some days he is
all fallen feathers
and downcast eyes

I am turrets and towers
and east facing windows

neither of us
is bearing roses

perhaps
if we were both
just a little more willing
to be wrong
for each other

Sarah A.

# I Am Doing the Best that I Can

I am doing the best that I can to be free of you.
I am neither your clone
Nor an extension of your identity.
I am not you and don't want to be you,
So do not impose your expectations on me.
I am the real me,
So get the hell out of my life if you cannot accept me as I am.

You will no longer control me,
Because I do not need you to be successful.
You will no longer crush my spirit,
Because I am loving and lovable.
You will no longer demean me,
Because I am good and worthwhile.
You will no longer punish me with guilt and shame,
Because I have forgiven myself.
You will no longer hurt me,
Because I am strong and persevering.
You will no longer send me into despair,
Because I see the light at the end of the tunnel.
You will no longer make me feel inferior, cowardly, weak and unworthy,
Because I believe in myself.

No matter what you say or do to me,
I am continuing on my journey of spiritual and emotional healing.
You will no longer be my source of conflict,
Because I am no longer your parasitic host.
I deserve happiness and inner peace,
Because I am an honest, lovable, caring, compassionate, good and
worthwhile person.
I am doing the best that I can to be me.

Sheryl M.

# The City 2

i left you somewhere between Bathurst and Spadina
at least that's where i left the conversation
my mind travelling down the loopholes and avenues
crawling along Bloor
we were groping
bricks
cobble stone
without shoes
we felt barefoot
you and i
utterly smashed
swinging the streets
pushing one another with words and laughter

has that feeling disappeared
been replaced
just been taken away for a while
forever
there is a drop of hell in that word

i can't tell you what my eyes say every time you splash against them
your image
my image of you.
i think there's something to be said for the fact that i've upheld it for so
long
perfect in its own way
fantastic

back then it was built around you
this cosmopolitan universe of touchstones
points of reference
conversation and conversion
points of interest and change
you were Cesare

it really is connect the dots with human beings
but i am a little tired of playing
and now i'd like to step back
and realize something
sobering
to get a glimpse of a bigger picture
that it's not just the hand of fate
at work on some abstract drawing
that was always far too complicated for me to grasp

Sarah A.

# My Side of Your Wall

There is a wall,
A big stone wall,
Tall, too tall to see over.
It separates you from me.

I know that you are there,
But I don't know how to reach you.
I started to take down this wall,
Reached out to you.

We touched for a moment
But you stepped away.
You broke contact
And started to rebuild your wall.

I am once again solitary,
Your wall
Too big, too strong,
To make it through.

We were together
For one beautiful moment.
We were one, and now we are two,
Each on different sides of your cold wall.

I hate it.
I hate that you built it.
I hate that you left me alone.
I hate my side of your wall.

I want to be on the other side of the wall with you.
But if you bring me with you,
I will surely die.
You will take away my freedom
That I have fought so hard to gain.

I want your wall to come down,
I want to be able to see you, touch you,
As we did in that one short moment.
But it seems as if we were never together.
I am alone,
On my side of your wall.

Justine N.

# Anxious love

After my lover's phone call
I think
'I was full and now I am empty'.
and the silence of this house is like steam
my movements are slow and distracted
for a moment afterwards
I struggle to find my page
again in the book
I was reading

Sarah A.

# Far Away Dream

Letting go,
Is it a far away dream?
Is it tangible?
Is it possible?
God, please help me.
I can't do it alone,
I fight it.

Forgive, accept, forgive, accept.
It wasn't my fault,
It wasn't his fault.
Does fault even matter?
It's just about letting go.
Your pain was so great,
Maybe greater than mine,
You had to hurt me.
We were both wounded.

But I've been carrying your baggage far too long,
Please God, help him,
Help me, help us.
Take this away so I can feel light.
Let light flow through me.
Please, release this pain.
It's not mine,
It never was.

Tricia C.

# Needle and Thread

How I miss you,
Your face as it is now,
Round, healthy.
Your arms around me,
Hands, holding hands,
Rough scarred hands of a man who has worked ragged,
Ragged, slow, drugged breaths.

You said you like my eyes glassy, pinned.
I looked pretty that way,
I always wanted to look pretty for you.
Pretty silly,
Pretty stupid,
Pretty fucking stoned.

Like the ripples in a pond from dropping a stone,
Our love expanded.
It hurt our families,
It hurt us,
It hurt,
I hurt.

Waiting for cars,
Cars with men,
Cars with money,
It hurt,
I hurt.

Until you came,
Until you said I was better than that,
But not too good for the needle.

Needle and thread,
There is a thread that sews me to you.

Suzanne C.

# The Game

When we met I worked with you,
Then over time a friendship grew.
Boy, we sure did rock that town,
From then 'til now, we've both calmed down.
We did some time on the inside,
Freed again and back to the grind.
Running hard, the sleepless nights,
The heavy sex, the senseless fights.
You went your way, I went mine,
Again we both were doing time.
In and out, revolving door,
There really must be something more.
Hooked up again and traveled west,
Adventures like I'd never guessed.
You showed me things I never saw,
Things that still have me in awe.
The way they move and shake out here
Has made me see things so crystal clear.
This place could hold much more for us,
More than just another bust.
Let's take this opportunity,
I'll help you and you'll help me.
Together we can ditch the scene,
So hold my hand, let's try this clean.

Karon B.

# Breaking Hearts

This pain within will not vanish,
Even with your words
Coated in displeasure.
The open fields where my voice once sang in peace,
Fences now surround,
Garbage is thrown.
My trust has been buried,
All to suit your throne.

Alessandra B.

# Married

I stand in the kitchen.
I'm going to walk out the door tonight.
I don't want to sit at home with you tonight.
You sleep, I can't sleep,
But I can't walk out the door.
I have nowhere to go.
But I guess that's really not true.
I have options, I have places to go,
But you aren't at those places.
We are home, you are in our bed.
There is nowhere I want to go.
It took me an hour of up and down the stairs to figure it out.
Stay awake, I ask. You tell me you can't.
You tell me you worked hard today.
But I don't like your answer—that's really the truth.
I'm needy and you are sleeping.
I really want to be mad and slam the door behind me as I walk out.
It feels good to be mad sometimes.
But it would only be good for a short moment,
And I'd realize you are still sleeping and all I want to be is at home.
So, I don't drive into the rain.
I go upstairs to bed, pull back the covers and crawl in.
You snore.
I watch TV and I am not alone.

Justine N.

# Outside Struggle

Fear, strength, tears, joy.
Loss, pain, happiness.
Discovering the reasons for escape,
Trying to overcome.
The same, yet so different,
Both kind, both scared.

He learns to cope, to understand,
Finding self, destroying vice.
He has never left his home, his stability behind.
He is strong, he is loving.

We bear resemblance to one another,
Yet our vices are only skin deep.
We laugh, we share tears,
We understand the recent hardship and deal only to survive.
We strive for humility and keep his secret ours.
He has become a true reflection of himself, not his father.
His nature is kind, but weakness is strong.
His emotions bear loss and lack of mourning.
He must celebrate his accomplishment and bury his own disapproval.

We suffered together, but silently until the tears,
Until we were unsafe.
We struggle on despite the cleanse.
Challenges are forever—we find gains in loss,
And strengths in loved one's weakness.
We bear mind to strength and anguish,
Attempting to rid challenges will never suffice.

No one has it easy, they would say,
No matter their appearance or grace,
No one has it easy.

Anonymous

# *Courage*

Someone rearranged the furniture.
I don't know why they would have done that,
After all it's my home not theirs.

I know I haven't been quick to organize things,
But it's only been a couple days, dammit.
Getting to decide what the home will look like
Is the best part of moving somewhere new.

Someone rearranged the furniture,
Right from under my nose.
I appreciate the help and all,
But it would have only taken a moment to ask me.

I know you probably had the best intentions,
But I really was OK on my own.
I'm starting to do more and more things by myself,
And was gaining self-esteem, a wonderful sense of accomplishment.

You walked in and didn't give me a choice.
You took that freedom away.
Maybe I wanted to try it myself,
To prove to myself I could do it,
To see how far I've really come,
But you squashed that goal.

And now I realize I'm done and over you.
I don't have to feel trapped by past memories,
I can move on to find my own happiness,
Limitless freedoms to nurture my soul,
To find out who I really am,
And discover a new way of living—
Not handcuffed to your memory,
Not squashed by your power.

Andrea E.

# Frank

I don't know how to put this.
I'm feeling lots of shame,
Not having gone out to search for him,
Only me do I have to blame.
But now my poor Franko is dead and gone.
I didn't get a chance to look him in the eye,
Say my last goodbye.
If he were only here today,
I'd say just how I feel,
I'd hold his hand, make him laugh,
And yes cook him his favourite meal.
Not now, it's way too late.
I guess he took sick and now there's only time for sorrow.
Now I must remember just one thing,
There may not always be a tomorrow.

Tammy L.

# Impotence

The significance of our silence

I want to get married
I tell Jack
putting down a pile of change
on a table I call 'my place of collected things'
the way giving something a title
bestows an aura of legitimacy
on what might otherwise be considered
a bloody mess

words
and our faith in them
that they are the location of truth
rather than arbitrarily assigned vessels
if that

what they carry
is nothing more
than an agreement to suspend our disbelief
to participate
in the abstraction of our hearts
to render our wants and needs
lofty ideals and moral philosophy
communicable

but in the silence between
my lover and I
is expressed
a tenderness
a soft sad love
for the fact of us
clinging to one another
choosing out of all of the things
in the universe
to cradle
through the deep uncertain hours of the night
we choose one
the other alternately
carrying each other
through the caverns of sleep
whispering with each exhale
dream with me
climb into my tomorrow
through the circle of my arms
meet me there
and I will kiss you
in the morning
over breakfast

Sarah A.

# Signs of Summer

There is ice cream in the freezer and ants crawling along the counter—as sure a sign of summer as I've seen all year.

The wind moans a low tune and the dogs prick up their ears as if a visitor might be calling, might be striding up my flagstone walk this very instant, curling their hand into a fist and knock, knock, knocking on my red front door.

It happened a couple of weeks ago—it was JW's—two by two they were—with pamphlets and hair tied back. So clean and neat it shamed me that I crouched behind my sofa listening to the hounds go mad. I had a bottle of Lysol in one hand and a cleaning rag in the other and I thought, just for a minute, that perhaps I ought to open up and tell them thanks but not for me please. But then they'd get that sweet holy smile and I'd feel compelled to tell them why. They'd answer back, trying to drag me down their saved path, and before you know it, my milk would be soured sitting in a glass on the counter and those damn dogs would have swallowed the left-over roast I was preparing to put in a sandwich. And after all that—I'd still be no closer to Jesus.

Gail M.

# A Prayer for Him

As I sit in here, I wonder, where is he?
Somewhere out there on crack.

Crack, the poison, the devil that once ruled me,
Is still ruling him.

God, bring him in.
Show him the power I have felt,
Give him faith and comfort.

Show him the strength I have now,
For it will help him.
He needs you more than ever.

He is in denial of you.
He runs from the help you give.
Why does he do this?

It's so clear to me now,
There is strength within you.
Share this with him before he wilts.

I believe, hope, and pray
He will find the serenity and courage
To come to sobriety, through you.

Lianne

# Anticipation

I'll tell you a secret if you tell me no lies, he said to her,
Desperation in his eyes,
Quivering with anticipation.
What on earth could it be? she thought.
The silence was killing her.
You could see the beads of sweat on his head.
His hands rubbing together nervously,
He rocked back and forth in the chair.
The seconds felt like minutes, minutes like hours.
I'll tell you a secret.
I'll tell you a secret!
What the hell did that mean?
The last six weeks have been incredible.
Why would I lie?
Her thoughts were whirling in her head.
No words were spoken just the squeaking of his chair.
Say it!
Tell me!
She screamed inside, her eyes pleading with him for the answer.
He took a deep breath and said,
I Love You.

Karen E.

# Sherry

Although it is reality
And it's how it must be,
I cannot seem to grasp
Your final relapse.
Cannot stop wishing you were here,
Although I know the truth is clear.
Cannot stop craving to hear
Your amazing laugh I hold so dear.
I want your sparkling eyes
Once again looking into mine.
I want to hear you say
You look beautiful today.
I want to do your dishes,
I want to grant your wishes,
I want to clean your bathroom,
Shining for when you come home.
I want to cook and make your lunch,
You'll like it, I have a hunch.
I want your breath in my ear
Holding me so near.
Even just to see your face,
Anytime, any place.
Just one more walk with Buddy and me,
This yearning I cannot deny.
To feel your presence, physically,
Would satisfy me for eternity.
One last laugh or kiss,
I would contritely exist.

Sheena S.

# Supposed to Be

I'll tell you a secret,
I thought it would be easy.
I thought you crawled, walked,
Went to school,
Stopped sitting on your Momma's knee,
Stopped asking questions,
Asking how? Why?
And when will I figure it out?

I thought it was natural.
But it's not,
It's hard,
And sometimes I cry.
It's too much,
More than I think I should have to carry.
You tell me this is life,
But I don't like it one bit.

You say, look around, look,
It's not bad.
I stop the sobs,
Lift my head from my hands
And look.
I look around at the accumulation of things,
Not things like furniture or clothing,
Things like people
And the feeling they bring with them.
I look at things like learning,

And possibilities that used to be impossibilities.
I forget about furniture and clothing,
They don't seem valuable,
Beside him, beside sisters,
And beside Moms and Dads.

When I'm scared, I can tell them a secret.
And it always seems so silly when you say it out loud,
You wonder why you held onto it so long.

You put it into their hands,
They put their lips together
And blow fear away.

Justine N.

# After the Rain

It looks as if it's going to be a beautiful day.
The sun is coming out.
There's a rainbow in the sky.
The birds are chirping,
Squirrels running, cats and dogs are playing,
Children are laughing,
People are puttering around their homes.
Spring is here!
It's a beautiful day in the city.

I miss my mom on days like today.
She loved the rain and especially after, when the sun would shine,
It would smell so fresh.
My mom used to wash our hair and clothes with rainwater,
She loved the fresh smell. So did I.

I have so many fond memories of our friendship.
If tears could build a stairway, and memories a lane,
I'd walk right up to heaven and bring you home again.
Always in my heart.
My mom was a tiny lady with a big heart.

Kim C.

# Tic-Toc

This is the way it's always been
In a room full of mini-me's
People who want to know
Why?
What?
When?
Where?

This is the way it's always been
To never quit quitting and wondering why
I have to be here
Why me, why us, why we?

This is the way it's always been
On the verge, the edge, close to tears
Run, hide, scream inside
I want to shout why me?
Because I am special?
Because I am blessed?
Because I have something to say?

This is the way it's always been
To fight for my right to be heard, my right to live
But maybe now, this won't be
The way it's always been

No coincidences means
Be here
Right now
To make people laugh, cry, feel, think
This is the way it's always been

Cold—hot—menopause
This is the way it's always been

I need to give
Men
A
Pause

This is the way it's always been
A timeline, an alarm, a clock
Tic Toc, Tic Toc

This is the way
It's always been

Michele I.

# My Path

There are moments in our lives when we find ourselves at a crossroads,
When we don't know which way to go.
I only see one path,
The road that takes me away from all the pain,
Away from all the suffering and the unknown.
I hate not knowing,
It scares me,
It makes me anxious.

I always expect the worst,
The premonition of something horrible,
And usually I'm right.
I worry about what to do
Or where I should be.
I feel as if I should be somewhere else,
With them,
By her side,
Taking care of her,
Nurturing her,
Loving her.

She won't be able to do it herself.
I want to tell her I miss her,
I want to tell her how much I love her.
If it weren't for her, I wouldn't know who I am.

She is my light.
She guides me in the right direction,
The path to greatness, success and laughter.
She makes me smile every time I see her.
I'm so grateful to have her.
Without her, I'm not myself.
What may happen to me without her?
That thought frightens me to the core of my being.
I will feel alone and sad.
She is special.
She is my sister.
She is my best friend.

Elaine W.

# Sweet Dreams

This is what whispers your name at night.
Memories ever so precious, ever so dear,
Moments of love and tenderness,
Held in your heart for all of your life.
The warm breath of my son while asleep in my arms,
Those first toddling steps forever engraved in my mind.
The love and support of a mother so dear,
The knowledge and wisdom of a wise, gentle father.
The strength of a grandmother, so like you.
The love of your life, softly breathing at night,
The sight of his face as you lay in his arms.
My prayers for my strength to keep going.
All of these things whisper to me at night.

Erin M.

# Friend

It's a treasure to have you around.
Oh, your laughs!
I don't have to know what you are laughing about,
I start laughing
Because I'm happy when you do.
It's so contagious.
When I'm busy, you help.
If I'm in trouble, you fix it.
When I cry, you calm me down.
In the summer you come by on your four wheeler,
In the winter you chop wood for the fireplace.
What would life be without you?
You're my friend.

Marga B.

# The Cottage

I came inside from sunbathing on the dock at my new cottage. How happy I am that I now have a beautiful, quaint cottage in the outskirts of Penetanguishene. The doors are so eccentric with purple accents.

The warmth from the sun has darkened my skin and warmed me enough to jump into the crystal blue waters of Georgian Bay. I came into the cottage to get a towel.

To my amazement someone had rearranged the furniture! I looked around to see if the girls, Selina and Jacquie, were inside and maybe were the ones who had paid someone to rearrange the furniture. But Jacquie's brand new silver Tiberson wasn't in front of the cottage.

I ran as quickly as I could throughout the cottage looking for the culprit. I peeked from one bedroom into another, just in case someone was in there. Maybe they would be surprised and run out.

Nope, no one was there.

Shit, I started to get frightened now, with the thought that someone had rearranged the furniture and was still in the cottage hiding.

I decided to go as quickly as I could to get some clothing on, because I was only wearing the teenie weenie bikini that Jacquie and Selina had bought me that was three sizes too small. They didn't think that I would have gained weight at Womankind the way I did.

Oh, there is my robe, yes. With a swift movement of my hands I threw on the robe.

I looked quickly to my right, then to my left. No movements yet.

Wait a minute.

I looked back and to my amazement someone rearranged the furniture back to where it belonged!

Yeah, behind the couch Jacquie and Selina jumped up and said "Gotcha Mommy!" What little buggers, all grown up and still like playing pranks on their mom.

"Last one in the lake is a dirty rascal," I shouted as I ran to the lake.

We all started giggling as we splashed in the water.

Ligia D.

# My Sons

No words can express how proud I am that you are my sons.
I thank the Lord for giving you to me.
When the day is done,
The things you have accomplished fill my heart with pride.
Watching you grow from boys to men,
It's a feeling I can't describe.
I knew you'd be someone amazing from the very start.
There is no greater joy in this world,
Than the love in a mother's heart.

Dianna D.

# Six to Ten

I remember the cherry-flavoured Popsicle juice dripping down my arm,
Climbing trees,
Playing hide and seek,
Learning to ride a bicycle.
I remember running so fast,
So fearless, so unaware.
What bliss!

I remember firecrackers,
Fresh cut grass,
Not a care in the world.
Memories playing like a slideshow in my mind,
A film about innocence.
I remember the pain when I fell and scraped my knee,
Time and time again,
Yet still never learning to slow down.
I remember snowstorms,
Which meant snow days filled by playing in our fairytale castles,
Eating the snow,
Icicles were lollipops,
What imaginations!
Beautiful.
No one could tell us differently or shatter our dreams.

I remember dogs barking and neighbourhood kids,
And looking both ways before crossing the street.
Where is that caution and common sense now?
Hurrying home as the street lights came on,

Cannot be out after dark.

I remember being picky at dinner and crying when there was no dessert,

Being scolded and knowing what I did wrong.

Where is that clarity now?

I remember nightmares and wanting to sleep in Mom's bed.

Where is that safety net now?

Christmas mornings filled us with raw excitement, pure ecstasy.

Where is our enthusiasm for life now?

We loved kittens and puppies and Saturday morning cartoons.

Now we can't even love ourselves.

Did we know so much more then?

Did we have so much more then?

Between the ages of six and ten?

Sheena S.

# To My Children

Just for this morning, I am going to smile when I see your face,
And I will laugh when I feel like crying.
Just for this morning, I will let you choose what you want to wear,
And I will smile and say how perfect it is.
Just for this morning, I am going to step over the laundry,
And I will pick you up and take you to the park to play.
Just for this morning, I will leave the dishes in the sink,
And I will let you teach me how to put that puzzle together.

Just for this afternoon, I will unplug the phone, keep the computer off,
And I will sit with you in the backyard and blow bubbles.
Just for this afternoon, I will not yell once when you scream for the ice cream truck,
And I will buy you one if it comes by.
Just for this afternoon, I won't worry about what you are going to be when you grow up,
And I will not second-guess every decision I have made as a mother.
Just for this afternoon, I will let you help me bake cookies,
And I will not stand over you trying to fix them.
Just for this afternoon, I will take us to McDonald's and buy us both a Happy Meal,
And I will give you both toys.

Just for this evening, I will hold you in my arms,
And I will tell you a story about how you were born and how much I love you.
Just for this evening, I will let you splash in the tub,
And I will not get angry.

Just for this evening, I will let you stay up while we sit on the porch,
And I will count all the stars with you.
Just for this evening, I will snuggle beside you for hours,
And I will miss my favourite TV show.
Just for this evening, I will run my finger through your hair as you pray,
And I will simply be grateful that God has given me the greatest gift.

I will think about the mothers and fathers who are searching for their missing children,
I will think about the mothers and fathers who are visiting their children's graves,
I will think about the mothers and fathers who are in hospital rooms watching their children suffer senselessly and screaming inside because they cannot handle it anymore.

And when I kiss you good night I will hold you a little tighter, a little longer.
It is then that I will thank God for you,
And I will ask him for nothing except one more day.

Love Always, Mom

Christine B.

# Ice Cream Summer

Summer, free time, no school, playing, helping mom.
Oh yeah, mom was always busy,
Especially in the summer, weeding the garden.

Today we have fresh strawberries,
Yummy, fresh out of the garden.
Oh, what a treat!

Get all my brothers and sisters,
Going to the forest to pick blueberries,
Each with his or her own container.
I picked two, one in my mouth and one in the container.
With blue tongues and lips, we came home.
Mom made jam with them.

Together picking blackberries,
Oh, those branches are so prickly!
Coming home with scratches on your hands and legs.
And of course a blue tongue.

But the best part of the summer was when the peas where ready.
We all sat together and peeled the peas, which was a day of work,
But we loved it.
We were paid with a huge ice cream topped with chocolate.
Mmm. Yummy.

Marga B.

# Mommy Can We Play?

Mommy can we play today?
Familiar words our children say.
Tomorrow we will find the time,
To build with blocks or sing a rhyme.
But think before we turn them down,
How quickly things they turn around.
Before we know it they are grown,
With busy lives all of their own.
So take the time now, do not wait,
Tomorrow it may be too late.
Listen when we hear them say,
Mommy can we play today?

Karon B.

# Lucas

My favourite moment was yesterday when I stopped by to see Lucas
And give him the socks and treats that I bought for him.
When he opened the door and saw that it was me,
His face lit up with joy.
He said, Mommy it's you,
And wrapped his arms around me.
His socks fit, which made me very happy.
He has been out of my care for so long,
When I was purchasing them at the store,
I didn't even know his shoe size.
I had to look at the socks and imagine his foot.
The socks fit him perfectly,
I felt maybe I wasn't such a bad mother after all.
In the snack mix I had made for him was dried mango,
Which my boyfriend had suggested.
I asked Lucas to try it.
He looked at it like it was gross,
Broke it in half and licked it.
Then, he made a face.
I immediately said, it's OK, I'll eat it,
And he said, no.
He put it back in the bag as if he just wanted to keep it,
Just because I had given it to him.

Jennifer C.

# Our Little Surprise

Walking around aimlessly and hopelessly,
Without a care,
I hope you'll always be there.
With you in my life,
I'll always share,
Forever tied together by fate.

We were careless,
But it's not a mistake.
For you this has always been a dream,
Now and forever we will be a team.
A little life inside me grows,
Boy or girl, nobody knows.
Blessed we are for such a gift,
I know this was on your bucket list.
Mom and Dad will be so proud,
Soaring on a little pink cloud.
Not great timing for our bundle of joy,
I want a girl, you want a boy.
Happy, healthy, ten fingers, ten toes,
One maybe two, hey, who knows?
I know you'll be a great dad,
Much better than the ones we had.
So we will have to wait and see
What this gift holds for you and me.

Jessica M.

# Mother's Day

This year marks the 10th Mother's Day without you.
I really don't know what to think, say or even do.
I remember 10 years ago when your magnolia just wouldn't bloom,
It missed you too
I think it's safe to assume.
There have been so many mixed feelings over the years,
Anger, laughter, confusion and a lot of tears,
Tears of sadness, joy and bittersweet freedom.
Acceptance for everything has started to come.
Although the path to get here has been long and hard,
And it hasn't been easy letting down my guard,
It's been so worth it, to be this new person.
With these old toxic ways you taught me, I'm more than done.
I kiss those painful memories goodbye,
And finally let go a deep and healing sigh.

Andrea E.

# *Neil Diamond*

Listening to Neil Diamond,
Even a lousy cheesy assed piece like tonight always makes her want to cry.
She doesn't know why.
Her mom loves Neil Diamond.
Maybe it has more to do with the memory of her mother's playfulness
Whenever N.D. would spin out a yearning, romantic, tortured tune.
Those rare moments when her mom would relax,
Sway and sing and let go of the pressures and race of her day.
Whatever it is, it gets her in the chest
And in the gut,
And right between the eyes.
A full body trigger.

Michelle V.

# I'll Tell You a Secret

I'll tell you a secret:
I don't really like myself.
I'm not sure why.
I never have.
I don't know what I did that was so awful,
Or what made me hate myself, but I do.
I have wonderful people around me
Who tell me how they love me,
But I just don't know why.
I want to be loved,
I want it more than anything in the world,
But I've always felt I loved others more than they loved me.
I've had friends hurt me so badly,
So badly that I don't want a close friend again.
Yet, at the same time, I do.
I am so afraid of being hurt.
I have so much pain inside,
I don't think I could handle more.
I've tried for seventeen years to figure out why he loves me,
Why he stays with me.
I know I'm not easy to live with.
I've tried pushing and pushing him away.
He never leaves, he always stays.
I have my precious daughter,
Who I wanted my entire life,
I can't even cope with the daily routine of raising her.
All she wants is a mom to play with her and spend time with her.
I can barely give her that.

I know I must learn to love myself before I truly love anyone else.
But how?

Jennifer G.

# ADVICE

# Just Go

When life takes you on a downward slope,
With abandoned goals, there seems no hope.
You ask yourself where to go from here,
And yet you stay just out of fear—
Fear of what will come with change,
To start things over somewhere strange.
All it takes is just to go.
I tell you this because I know.
And whether you go near or far,
You will thank your lucky star
You listened to your inner voice.
To change your life is just a choice.

Karon B.

# Lake or Water

As far I can see, only water,
Calm, peaceful.
The sun just above the lake
Gives the water a warm red glow,
So beautiful, so peaceful.
A boat comes by, the water starts to move,
Another boat flies by, the water makes waves,
Still calm and peaceful.
If there are many boats,
The water isn't peaceful anymore,
It gets restless and polluted.

A human is composed mostly of water.
If we have too many boats in our mind,
Boats like stress, negative thoughts, loneliness or pain,
Our mind gets restless and polluted.
That creates addiction.
There are places where the water is calm and peaceful.
Our task in life is to find that calm and peaceful water,
And sit on the edge of that lake.

Margo B.

# *Justice*

There is a bee that has been trapped inside of my house for days
he buzzes in aggravation
no longer afraid of his proximity to us
makes violent death spirals
towards our heads
banging furious against the glass

he wants to be killed
and although I won't feed him
melting sugar cubes slowly in my tea
I refuse to play the hand of God
imagining
in a cruel entirely human way
that he did something deserving of his fate

Sarah A.

# Names

I don't trust anything that repeats itself
With the consistency of a well thought out lie

Perhaps I feel safer
with glittery omissions
Because the things our mentors fail to mention
Are the ones that sting
And fade
Once you've figured out
What was missing
For yourself
And in the silent place
consider
How one day you will begin
moving backwards
To ashes and dust
And how you can't really hold on to anything
Though you spend your whole life gathering
For yourself,
For the children of your hope and regret
and the children of their kindness
who can never out live their names
though they may grow old and accustomed to them
wear them into such a comfortable fit
And uniqueness

We can't take them with us
We go
They stay
With elaboration

Sarah A.

# HOPE

# Dear Alcohol

You crept slowly into my life,
Then my soul you took as your prize.
You convinced me you were my only friend,
But now it's time to say goodbye.

I'm no longer going to hurt my children.
They're getting their mother back!
No more lies, cheating and hiding,
So get your bags and pack!

I'm no longer going to hide my feelings,
And I'm getting rid of guilt and shame.
No more isolation and embarrassment,
No more playing your stupid head games.

I'm no longer using you for confidence,
I am regaining my self-esteem.
No more blackouts and memory loss,
No more stealing away my dreams!

I'm no longer hurting my mental health.
And physically, I'm going to be fit!
No more interfering with my medication,
So go!
I no longer like you, not even a bit!

You are no longer allowed in my life.
My regained soul is mine to keep.
I'm reconnecting with my family.
So long, alcohol, you're nothing but a creep!

Jeanne L.

# *Faith*

I wake and breathe the morning air.
It used to be hard to wake up some mornings;
I didn't want to start the day.
I'd stay under the covers,
Wait until everyone had left for the day.
It seemed too hard,
It seemed like the world had fallen in on me,
I had no idea how to climb out of the rubble.
I thought it would never end.

Even after I had brushed the dust away,
It seemed like it would never stop coming,
Pushing me backward no matter how hard I pushed forward.
The world is against me,
It never gets easier.
It pushes you down,
You are never strong enough to make it stop,
Never.

I cried over this a lot.
I cried about how unfair this world is,
But I was tired of that too—
Tired of fighting and crying out to the world to leave me alone.

But I've learned something
Or found something
I never knew I had.
It's called faith.
It takes the weight off your bones.
I trust, instead of accusing this world of being cruel.
I found the words—it will all be OK.
I used to say those words when I was seventeen and nothing ever felt so heavy,
And now I can say them and it all doesn't seem so bad.

Justine N.

# My Destiny

The grey clouds are lifting,
Like a thousand pounds off my shoulders.
The grey clouds are lifting,
The sunshine is beginning to pour through.
Its bright white-yellow rays are revealing a path,
The path to my recovery.
This journey has long awaited me,
For sobriety and recovery is my destiny.
I deserve recovery.
I am worth recovering.

It's been ten years.
I lived a life of darkness,
With this grey cloudy haze always following me.
I thought I was destined for death,
Destined to live that life of pain, fear, depression.

I have come to realize that the day when those grey clouds lifted,
They unveiled my fate—my recovery.

Finally, my time has come.
My time to shine bright and be strong is here.
I am destined to be sober and clean,
I am destined to feel whole.
I feel at peace with myself.
I have longed for the day when I could express myself.
I have found me.
That beautiful young lady looking back at me in the mirror,
This is me.
I haven't seen her in years.
She was a lost soul.
It's been a long journey,
But every step was worth it.
I now can accept myself for who I am.
I surrendered.
I now have peace and serenity every moment of my life.

Kate D.

# Alive and Beautiful

The sky has opened up.
I can see the bright blue sky,
Wanting to pour into the darkness,
The darkness that has been keeping me in a dark place.
I can already feel the sunshine on my face,
And the warming in my body and my soul.
I feel a small light from the inside,
It wants to burst through me,
Like the most beautiful sunshine,
And start anew, full of energy and happiness.
I feel a warmth inside me,
I want to share it with the world.
I want to be like a spring flower,
Slowly coming into the light,
Blossoming into God's beautiful creation.
I am bright and cheerful,
I am fragrant and beautiful,
And people look at me in awe because of my beauty.

God put me on this earth to be appreciated and loved,
People look at me and they smile.
They love what they see,
Admire the vibrant person who is full of life,
And wants to give love and compassion to everyone she touches.

Barb H.

# Assertive Boundaries

I draw a line, but sometimes it feels like it's in the sand.
I try to be strong with my boundaries and limits,
But mostly I crumble and collapse under the pressure.
My good intentions, integrity and purpose flow down the drain,
Along with my self-esteem and any glimpse of growing assertiveness.

I sit alone gathering my courage,
Vowing not to let them affect me this time,
Wanting to sit in solitude with my strength,
Loving myself, being happy with who I am.
But isolation is a scary place,
My mind can play many tricks on me,
And sometimes that mountain I'm creating,
Is really only a grain of sand.

I draw a line to protect and preserve who I am.
I resolve that no one is worth compromising for anymore.
I gain happiness and contentment within myself.
I focus on being good to myself and others.
I know that I am kind and loving,
I deserve to be treated with respect.
I will not succumb to fear and hurt.
Anger will no longer take over my life.
I am strong, I am worthwhile.

Things aren't always as bad as they are in my head.
While I reach out to find that common ground,
I will stand firm by that line
That I have now drawn in concrete.

Andrea E.

# Bottle That

I'm feeling conflicted and confused,
Yet self-assured and encouraged.
It's all perspective.
If I'm feeling stressed, every little thing will set me off,
And I feel as if the world is collapsing down around me,
One domino at a time, crumbling in ways I can't stop.
Yet, at times I can feel on top of the world,
Realizing the scope of everything going right,
Focusing on the positive things said,
Not the worthless, fat, piece of shit ones.
I remind myself of the calm, fuzzy feelings,
Not the knife in my heart, I can't breathe ones
Thinking of gratitude
For all that's been brought into my life,
Not the hopeless frustration for the things I don't have.
I want to bottle that feeling,
The one where your whole body is so calm,
Your thoughts are at peace,
And you can feel the air around you,
Just clinging to you, grasping,
Trying to get you to stay in that moment—
That moment that can't be bottled.
And once it's gone, it's only a fleeting memory,
Of what was, but more importantly, what can be again.
Those moments come more frequently if I let them,
Although they are still so unfamiliar.
I have hope that one day those moments I want to bottle
Will once again outnumber those moments I want to smash, burn and
destroy.
Hope.
I have found it.
And I will hold on,
Until it's in abundance once again.

Andrea E.

# My Groupie Heart Beats

I almost collapsed when he said my name during a song. I looked over to her and smiled. I had died and gone to groupie-heaven. Life really wasn't ever going to get any better, and it didn't for a long time. It went down long before I could turn it around.

I won't forget those hot summer nights when I was 15. It was a summer somewhat like now, hot, sticky nights with less rain. There was never a need for a sweater, never the need to cover up. Anyway, the less we wore, the more we gained. How could anything beat the life I was living? She and I had latched onto this up-and-coming local band. Or at least we thought they were up-and-coming. It didn't matter what the rest of them said. It didn't matter that artistic egos were rearing their ugly heads. The faces of those large egos were beautiful enough to distract us from every truth. We had always wanted to be groupies; we wanted to be with the band. In our denim minis and tiny tops, we were going to make sure they didn't miss our presence. I read about groupies, about young girls in love with larger-than-life rock stars. They were in it for the music, and so was I.

But it was dangerous to love these wanna-be rock starts. And it felt just as dangerous to love my idols from 1967. Young girls were as disposable as the shirts they wore on stage; half unbuttoned before the show even started and thrown into the crowd by the end of the night. But this was our life, hanging on to every word, every hip thrust from centre stage. In our little world of funk shows and boys, nothing was ever going to be better than sneaking drinks behind bartenders and dancing front and centre at every show.

We made friends with the ex-girlfriends who were more than willing to share details. We were young and naïve, harmless enough to be privy to secrets. They shared their designer makeup and insider information. We were on guest lists at big clubs in the city. I was talking our way into any bar with my big attitude and name drops. There were late night parties that lasted until the sun came up.

I'll never forget the first time I saw someone do drugs. We sat having a conversation at the coffee table in a tiny apartment in Toronto. He turned to me and said simply "Do you mind if I do a line?" He didn't offer me anything, it was as casual as "Do you mind if I smoke?" Instead of feeling as if I was in the wrong, I knew I had found my home. It was all I had ever imagined with the boys, the beats, the drinks and joints. This was as close to the groupie life as I was ever going to get. I loved every minute.

I chased those sweaty hot summer nights and chased parties and cocktails straight into someplace dark where there was no music. I chased the music and the band until I was chasing the drinks and drugs. I was chasing each party in hope of another drink, another drunk. The music had faded, the band fallen apart and all there was was me, alone, sitting with another drink chasing another drunk.

I hadn't even made it to 19. I was now starting my day crying into my drink, wondering where I went wrong, wondering how the chase had led me to this. Something happened between the music and the day I woke up but I was caught in the middle, too blinded to notice. I was in pursuit of my teenage dream. That dream led me into this nightmare. I didn't know where I was, how I got there or how the hell to get back. My new dream or delusion had me chasing the hope that each time it was going to be different. It was going to be like it used to be in the bright lights of the front row.

My teenage crushes had come back to our hometown to play a pseudo-reunion show. But there was no summer heat, it was the dead of winter. I arrived in tall shoes and a little top. I waltzed into the club as I had many times before. A couple years older, with new friends and a bottle of tequila, I didn't last long. I didn't head for centre stage. I headed for the bathroom with my bottle of tequila. After only minutes inside, I was being escorted back to the curb. I stood in the cold as they poured out my bottle. My heart broke as I watched the amber liquid run into the drain.

Somewhere between the hot summer when I was 15 and this cold winter, the music was no longer what was important. It was thrown to the wayside in favour of something else. That bottle was now what was important. I felt it held the secret. It had what I needed to be okay. But as I got to the bottom of each bottle, I was just as empty and lost as before. I stood in the cold that night broken hearted. After, I tried to find solace in a pill. But that didn't fix my broken heart either.

I sat with that empty heart and kept trying to fill it with booze and substances. That was the only thing I knew. I thought that the only thing to mend my broken lonely heart was to hide, drunk at home. It wasn't working anymore. My solution had failed me and that was the scariest part of all. I knew now that something else had to be out there. Something had to make me feel better. You can't live like that.

I was found eventually, pulled from my hole by people who had been there before. They are the only ones who know how to go in and get you out, and still come back unscathed. That was the end, or maybe more like a beginning.

Last month I sat on the lawn at an open air concert watching my new favourite musician. In his tight white pants and cut-off tee, he wailed on his blues guitar. I was still in groupie-heaven. I closed my eyes and remember exactly the feeling my groupie heart gets when he plays. It beats to the sound of the music just as it used to. My old crushes walked past and I realized that nothing had really changed. I still want to chase boys in bands. I just got lost somewhere along the way. I just got lost on the way when the drink became more important than the music and the boys in the bands.

I am in it for the music.

Justine N.

# The Gift of Silence

I find the silence very hard. It is deadening to my soul.
But silence can be a wonderful thing:
Peace, serenity, just my thoughts,
No idle chattering, no blaring horns,
No television, no phone,
A gift to yourself to be cherished.
Memories, pleasant or not, flood my mind.
Silence can enhance your senses:
The smell of freshly oiled furniture,
A view of a serene lake,
The feel of soft suede,
The taste of warm bread,
The melody of a piano.
Silence evokes memories, good and bad.
Silence is a rare gift that we do not often give ourselves.
I should take more time to permit myself this gift.
Although unlikely, it should become part of my daily regimen.
Silence is a scrapbook of my life,
a candle flickering in the wind that disappears all too quickly.

Erin M.

# Choices

I remember when I felt free to make my own choices,

And I was confident they would be beneficial to my life and those around me.

I long for the freedom of responsibility

And the peace that comes with it, even in the midst of chaos.

I remember when I was strong,

When everyone could count on me to be there and follow through.

Honesty was my constant companion,

Along with trust and perseverance in all I did.

I remember the peace I had in my soul, no matter what chaos surrounded me.

I remember when I loved myself,

Without needing validation from others.

I long to be free again.

Anne R.

# *Colours*

The grey clouds are lifting and the sun is shining in.
There's a twinkle in my eye
As I breathe in the slightly damp air,
I feel it through my body like a spirit passing through me,
Reminding me the grey clouds are lifting.

I have been stuck in those clouds for way too long.
But now I see what I've been missing.
So, on those grey days I dream of what could have been,
What has been, or what will be
In the next episodes of my life.

The fog is lifting and the greyness is disappearing.
Finally I feel like me again.
Strangely, I had forgotten who me was.
But now the skies are opening and the sunlight heats my body,
A burning sensation.
A few clouds take their time,
Spitting down drops of rain,
Spiritually cleansing my body.

The grey clouds are lifting in my head and in my heart.
I don't have to hide,
I don't have to cry,
This is me and I accept that, with every up and down I take,
My world is now full of colour,
No more grey.

Alessandra B.

# Right Here, Right Now

My heart feels free being on my own
With the world ahead of me,
A wonderful life before me.
I've had to struggle to find my own way,
No thanks to you.

But I have faith today that I've never known,
And know I don't have to go back,
As scary as moving forward may be.

It's my journey, my path,
And I can do it.
I'm worth trying for,
Not for anyone else, but me.
You can't tell me how to act or think anymore.

I feel like a bird soaring high,
Going where I want to go,
Doing what I need to do,
And loving myself,
For the first time ever.
Loving myself,
And giving myself credit.

Although it hasn't been easy,
Every smile is worth the preceding tear,
And every breath of serenity is worth
All the anxiety I've had to overcome.

Finally free to breathe,
Be calm,
Still in my heart.
Happy to be me,
And more proud than ever.

This is a wonderful journey,
And I'm grateful for every moment
That leads me to be right here, right now.

Andrea E.

# Freedom To Heal

Life is given to live, not to take.
There's a ship in the harbour,
But that's not what ships are for,
Just as our bodies are our temples, sacred beings,
We are not made to cause ourselves pain,
Though it may briefly feel good.

Change is the only constant, which is hard sometimes,
But if you take a grain of sugar from every little setback,
You will have a little more headspace to teach and be taught.

One day clean is better than none at all.
I would like to be free from all this mayhem,
From these shackles that keep me down.
I refuse to be held captive,
My will is too strong.
We have just one life and I want to be free.

Alessandra B.

# My Feelings

I can love again,
As long as I try to love myself first
So I can love others.
My feelings have been hurt badly.
I've been walked on, shit on, put down.
But now I can walk with my head high.
I now have people in my life who love me
And who tell me that I am good
And I can do it,
And the pain will still be there
But it will go away one day.
I will not hear them say those things anymore.

Tammy

# *Pride*

it is not only human to want to escape
every animal has an instinct
that tells it to avoid being trapped
to resist a mentality of captivity for as long as possible
call it hope
call it integrity
proud naked men parade
one without an arm
daring to bare his every imperfection so casually in the light
and not asking for anyone's sympathy
how dare he not be a cause
i am a verb conjugated by the city
it extrapolates me
it has it's own logic and wisdom
its own derivatives and derivations
my eyes on my own reflection distracted
by the crowd at yonge and dundas square
where police men throw arms around one another
in front of a big screen
that lit Vancouver
though Rob Ford
will always always support hockey games
because brutality makes for a better cameo

Sarah A.

# *Mandalas of Hope*

Feelings, now I'm here.
Loneliness—I'd love to call my husband.
I did not think I would.
Now I look forward to calling him tomorrow.

Feelings, now I'm here.
Connections, friendship.
I'm so happy that Susy is here; we write together.
I'm going to buy something like Sarah is wearing because that's my style.

Man, I'm doing this in English,
I'm surprising myself.

Feelings, now I'm here.
There is so much creativity in me and after these five weeks,
I'm going to let it all out.
There is glass waiting to be stained and cut,
Mandalas to be coloured and so much more.

No time for drinking.

Marga B.

# I didn't know

I learned when I was six
That this world could be a sad place.
I was too young to recognize the lesson then.
Maybe I should have,
Playing with my baby sisters
In the funeral home
At the foot of my Opa's coffin.
I stood up,
Looked at his pale face
And ran my hand along his cheek.
He was still my Opa
Even though it was only his body left behind.

I know that sadness now
When I think of everything I have missed,
Everything my mother missed
Losing her father at 32.
I was oblivious then.
I don't remember a tear.
I know now that we would have been close.
It is only now in my twenties
That this loss has the most impact.
It's only now that life seems unfair.
I watch people grow ill.
It's the things we might miss.

But I can't spend time
On those types of thoughts.
My faith in God doesn't tell me
That everyone will be okay.
It tells me
Those left behind will get through the pain.

Justine N.

# I Almost Used Today

I almost used today.

689 days clean and the pain felt too great to bear.

The overwhelming challenges of life and trying to live clean

Snuck up and threatened to smother me this morning.

Scared and alone, I sat in my room with tears soaking my face.

Paralyzed to move forward,

Obsessing over the consequences if I took that first step back.

Crazy paranoia and a nosebleed reminded me of what was waiting,

But my head still told me I wasn't strong enough to face the pain of the day.

The internal struggle between my addiction and faith was bitter.

For a few brief moments, I turned my back on God and was plunged into the darkness.

All around me I could see no light, no hope.

Terrified and alone, I cried out, part fear, part faith.

I was reminded, pain is not the enemy, fear of passing through the pain is the enemy.

The pain will go away if given the chance to heal.

Those words, like my lighthouse at the edge of the cove,

Led my way back out of the dark.

As I rubbed my eyes adjusting to the light,

I noticed my toolbox at my feet.

There lay phone numbers to call,

Personal affirmations to say,

Literature to read,

Paper to write.

And I felt warmth in my heart again,

A small amount of courage reminding me,

I don't have to use, no matter how dark times may get.

I am OK, I am strong enough to get through life's challenges,

No matter how insurmountable they may seem.

I can let go of old thoughts that keep me stuck in old patterns.

I am fully in charge of my own happiness.

So if you are struggling today,

Reach out and find your lighthouse,

For we all have one of our very own,

Just waiting for us to come home out of the dark.


Anonymous

# The Light

She sits in her desolate room,
No music, no lights,
Just anger
And her thoughts,
To run away forever,
As far as she can go,
Where maybe she won't remember
This shitty town and how it's treated her.

The corruption in her mind,
Blinded from all the smoke,
With only a hand to feed off,
For those who have something to offer,
A quick high, another pill to pop,
They'll do anything to get you hooked.
They don't care.

It will be a long hard road,
But if she can just hold on,
Just get by,
Focusing on her life,
Ignoring those who want her for what she's not,
She knows what she is able to accomplish.
She knows this,
And those who are left in the ditch,
Away from the light,
May look at her one day
And think what they could have done,
If only they saw the light.

Alessandra B.

# *In My Day*

In my day,
If we got stuck in a ditch,
We got out and pushed.
There is a logical order to accomplishing things,
Not whining or complaining
Like a newcomer at a meeting
Not living in the solution,
Not realizing that taking responsibility is the first step to feeling better.

Nobody really has God on speed dial
But if I did,
He would tell me to get out and push.

The solution is actually doing the work
Not talking about it
Because that is just an over-worked lame excuse.

I remember doing my inner child work
And a gal came in and said to the executive director,
I can't do this.
I wish I could have pulled her aside and said,
Nobody forces you to relive your trauma unless you opted for criminal court.
Only you have the power to say what YOU want to say.
You will hear the solution to your pain here.
Use that to comfort yourself.
Why live in pain
When the solution is as simple as getting outside your fear
And doing the work?

The work is to find comfort in new ways
So you don't feel so scared all the time.
I think it is fear of fear
That stops women from doing this process of self-examination.
Trying something new and different is only as hard as YOU make it.

I don't want to feel bad inside,
I just want some relief from the pain,
Just like everybody else does.
My solution is to re-parent my inner child,
Softly and gently recreate my inner strengths.
I have to get outside of myself and push the bad feelings away.

If I get stuck in a ditch,
I have to get out and push
And get snot and tears and guck in my face,
Just to stay clean and out of trouble.

I wish I didn't have to hurt like this
But that is like denying being human
Or a bit like saying
My farts don't smell
Or I never burp
Or I don't know
Or I don't want to feel stupid
Or awkward or lonely or needing others.

This is the human condition,
Every emotion of the rainbow to experience or endure.
Your choice,
Your life.
And if by chance, you should happen to call me friend,

I shall hold you in my arms and let you know
It is okay to be you
As you are exactly at this minute.

April A.

# Continue on the Journey

The mental image of spring is so incredibly soothing.
Just thinking of the heat from the sun,
The smell of new blossoms and grass,
The rustling of the leaves in the breeze,
The animals nurturing their young,
The spring rain and the long days
Exude an outpouring of warmth and serenity from every pore in my body.
All is new, fresh, untainted—reborn.

That's how I feel today.
My spring is just around the corner.
I am rising up from the darkness toward the sun like the crocus and the daffodil.
I am singing like the birds.
I am coming out of hibernation.
I am being reborn.
A new chapter of my life is beginning.
I will soon soar with the eagles.

This time, life will be different.
No more doom and gloom,
No more sadness, no more guilt and shame,
No more fear.
My life will be rich with the hope, courage, goodness,
The worthiness and love that make up spring.
The wafting of the flowers in the breeze,
The chirping of the squirrels and the cooing of the doves
Echo the blossoming warmth, happiness and peace within me.

I cherish this new life.

Never do I want winter or anything else to take it away.

I've let the darkness in all too often before.

This time I travelled a new road, one that led me to a spiritual renewal.

This oneness of mind, body and soul with the universe,

It is swelling within me like a tsunami.

Life is getting better every day, with each small step forward.

Riding the road to spring doesn't have to be seasonal.

All one has to do is continue on the journey,

The journey of infinite spiritual blossoming,

For spring to be eternal.

Thank you Lord for thinking about me. I'm alive and doing fine.

Sheryl M.

# The Skies Above

I am doing the best I can.
Wait, should I be doing this?
This doesn't make any sense,
I was doing my best when I was using.
What a Catch 22.
I scream and I shout to the heavens above,
Show me a sign,
I am so lost on this earth.

I am doing the best I can.
Yet everyone thinks it's a crock of shit.
How would they know what my best is?
I am here to do what I need to do,
Whether it leads me to my righteous path
Or leaves me to glare at the skies above.
I am doing the best I can.

Some days, my mother would tell me
The twinkle in my eyes has gone.
Then one day she looked at me, clean and sober, and said,
Your twinkle is back, I'm so proud of you.
Damn, that feels good.
I think I'm finally starting to believe that my true self is coming back,
And no one can take that away from me.
Sitting on a cot in my jail cell, thinking about nothing and everything,
I thought to myself,
I am doing the best I can.

Ten years of this bullshit and I'm done.
I did the best I could when it needed to be done.

Alessandra B.

# Rebirth

This is my summer voice.

I yell to the sky, I pound my fists on the ground.

My summer voice carries me through the wind, below the willows.

My heart's content with the beads of sweat dripping down my back.

They speak, but I do not hear.

Scream louder, they said, but my voice was gone,

Caught up in the willows, where they talked amongst the trees.

As I slowly left, my voice returned, a weight off my shoulders.

It's been so long, but my true self has wandered home,

Through the earth and back into my soul.

I can now be one with my surroundings and sing as loud as I can.

The man on the corner starts to play his harmonica,

Taking all my doubts and fears away,

As we would dance and sway to our summer voices.

Sing and dance as if no one's watching.

Your mind will take you to places you could never have imagined.

This is my summer voice.

I'm listening, but I am lost.

Come back to me, spirit, fill my heart with love.

You will never get this chance again.

This is my summer voice.

Clear your mind and yell up to the mountaintops.

Be your own light, and let it shine for everyone else to see.

This is my summer voice.

Alessandra B.

# Walls of Sorts

Knocking down walls,
I trudge through my past
To protect the world, and myself,
From seeing what I'm really all about.
There are some deep, dark parts of me
I don't even know.
But slowly, one after another,
They've been revealing themselves lately.
I don't know if I'm completely ready
To knock down all the walls that have been built,
But like it or not, they seem to crumble anyway.

Scared to move forward
But too hurt to move back,
I feel I'm in limbo of sorts,
But at least I'm feeling today, right?
Not trying to numb away the pain,
I'm trudging through it,
Knocking down, working past the obstacles I come across.

Knocking down walls,
I imagine exploring old Italy.
My heart longs to travel,
To be in a foreign land with the Christmas bells.
Do I go somewhere warm with sandy beaches?
Or go exploring ancient history?
Relaxation and adventure await me,
On the other side of that plane trip.

I've knocked down the walls, the old beliefs,
Telling me that I can't succeed, that I don't deserve it.
I've climbed over the rubble that was once engrained in me,
I've started to search for new truths.
Believing I can do it, I deserve success,
Finally my dreams are starting to come true
In ways I thought would remain forever fantasy.
This is really my life?
This is what I'm building,
So I need to nurture it and treasure it,
Instead of knocking down the walls of success.

Andrea E.

# My Emancipation

I felt sad after he left.
He was my hope,
My saviour,
My co-dependent lover.
As the rain came down,
I knew I would be okay
Because God gave me grace to face life
Without a lover.
I don't need external validation
To feel okay inside.

I look out over the city,
The Rammstein fire still aflame in the distance.
I will always remember our passion,
What hope he brought to my life.

It feels good to be soaked.
It quenches the thirst inside for love.
No barbecue tonight on my penthouse floor.
Alone with a Higher Power
Showing me the Beauty of the Hammer.
My 15 kilometre walks in awe of what the rain nourishes.
The rain helps me appreciate the sunny days,
How I can live without a man—freedom at last.
My tears fall gracefully, as gracefully as the sky.
The pain is healthy and cathartic,
As natural as God's rain.
I will be okay.
I can do this.
I don't have to listen to Patriarchal talk any longer:
"You should, you could, you would,
And stop starting all your sentences with 'I'," he said.
Fuck you, Joe, Moe and Larry.
Go to Hell.
And the rain just kept pouring down, exactly as it should.

April A.

# Finding Me

What if the life I imagine were really true?
What if all my hopes and dreams weren't simply that?
What if there was a world where my dreams were the reality I lived?
I'm getting glimpses that they may not be just dreams anymore.
I am terrified, paralyzed with little glimmers of that wonderful hope and faith.
Good things are coming in at a rapid pace
Much like the child who starts rolling the snow ball
It starts off small and grows as it gains momentum
Until it really takes on a life of it's own
I fear I won't know what to do with these good things
For so long I cowered in the darkness
Snuggling close to my low self esteem
And self imagined failures
Listening to the lies that were forced down my throat
Believing them as truth
Until broken and tired I just wanted to give up
And like a beacon of light I was led out of that dark place
And into a life far more then my dreams could have imagined.
Dream job? She has it. Wonderful home? Found that too. Writing aspirations coming true before her eyes and happiness abounds.
Shattering those lies I was fed.
Standing strong in courage.
Facing the life that has been waiting for me
Yet I stall
Afraid of what to do with success
For so long it's been the most unfamiliar
And I'm supposed to accept this new reality
That good feelings are true
Happiness is okay
And the success is hard earned and deserved
I have to accept me.

Andrea E.

# Eyes of a Child

I am afraid of nothing.
Life is full of change.
We go day to day looking,
Trying to stop the rain.

The sun comes out,
We stop and pause
To see just where we've been.
We are surprised that the circle came
Back to the beginning again.

Each day is filled with the same routine,
We try to look for more.
We pack the car and grab the kids,
To head out for the store.

Toys and clothes, the Chinese crafts,
Fill the car full to the brim.
We think what a waste of time this is,
There's enough junk at home to smother us all.
The kids laugh and mom sighs,
At least we have each other.

As we race through life we wonder,
What is the Human Race?
When do we reach the finish line?
How do we set the pace?

The universe will guide our way
With a higher power, they say.
I think it's a tree in flower or bee,
Maybe I'll learn one day.

Always reaching for the sun,
Just as nature taught us,
We work, we strive, we run to show the world
We know how to do it.
The path is long,
The road is steep,
And all we want to do is sleep.

It's hard, it's tough but we are strong.
Life is meant for living.
When we think we have it right,
The horizon changes direction.
Then we're left to stop and think,
What is my connection?

When I feel that life is over,
There's nothing left that's fun,
The eyes of a child guide my way,
And my life has just begun.

Garaldeen

# Butterflies

Knocking down walls,
I bust them down.
It hurts, but I do it anyway.
I know deep inside that I want to be free of my addictions,
But my walls are the saviour of my hurt little girl inside.
I want to diminish these demons and be free.
I want to sway like a bird over the sea,
I want to not have a care in the world.
I want to see from above all before I vanish into a caterpillar,
Gone in the dust.

I ended up in Alice In Wonderland,
I am a smoking caterpillar.
I climb the highest tree to the very top,
It smelt like luscious pine.
I make my way to the top,
I find a rattled branch,
I start to make my cocoon.
I realize I am building my walls up again.
I am scared to be left there alone
While I become a beautiful butterfly,
Because of evil predators.
I hatch and realize it wasn't so bad after all.
After knocking down all my walls,
I am now a confident, beautiful butterfly
That sways free over the sea.

Emily L.

# When the Earth spoke

I listened when the Earth spoke.
It rumbled through the floor boards,
Loud, commanding, forcing me to open my ears.

I had ignored its warnings before.
Quiet vibrations, calming movements beneath my bare feet.
I'd close my ears,
Feel the movement in my toes,
Feel it through my small frame,
Just a soft cry from the Earth.

It was different now.
The Earth spoke loud, too loud to ignore.
Still frames on the walls of the house shook.
They dropped to the floor; shattered glass flew across the room.

I told you to listen, said the Earth.
I told you to make preparations.
I told you this would happen.
I told you the ground would move and your world would shake.
Walls would crack,

ceilings would fall in
and leave you standing in the rubble.
You could have walked away.
You could have brought your things to a safer place, a sturdier place.
You could have listened to me,
listened to the words being spoken by the shakings in the ground.

I could have left.
I could have walked away.
I could still walk away.
Maybe you are testing my faith,
Testing to see how strong I really am.
I am strong. I stand amongst the broken walls.
I made my choice to stay.

Justine N.

# *Mirror*

One day I stopped and looked in the mirror.
I did see a person who I resembled
But who looked nothing quite like me.
I wondered who this person was
Who looked back at me today.
She has new clothing on her body,
And the cleanest hair that I've seen.
I realized with my own eyes
That in the mirror was me.
I see the change in me.
Thank the Lord I am alive this day,
And in the end for the truth that it is me,
My Best Friend indeed.

Christine H.

# Drug of Choice

Hello Drug of Choice,
I just want to say that I will not require your services anymore.
The side effects of your medication proved to be very toxic to me,
Very toxic physically, mentally and spiritually.

My family does not like me while I'm medicated.
I make them feel angry, afraid, lonely, worried, disgusted and helpless.
I do things that I am ashamed of.
It makes me lose my memory and say things that I don't mean.

I throw up when I brush my teeth
And I shake unless I have more.
I miss time from work because I don't feel well without it,
Yet I can't function with it.

It's no longer a cure for me.
I have also tried your alternative medicine.
That doesn't work either.

Thanks for trying, but I found another healer,
It is much more effective and a lot cheaper.
My recovery is slow and painful,
But it's working.

So long Drug of Choice,
I'm leaving you today.

Goodbye, Goodbye, Goodbye . . . Barb.

Barb H.

# Recovery

The task ahead of us is never as great as the power behind us.
I now know about life and all the opportunities it has to offer.
The wonder of change is exciting,
Like the dawn of a new day.
That's what it becomes,
The fresh air smell in the spring.

I have started my journey to recovery.

The beautiful stars that shine at night
I now watch with delight.
Dreaming of new ways,
Enjoying the pleasures of walking and playing in the park,
I am more grateful for the green grass,
The shining sun,
Or even the rain, as it beats down hard.
It's like the sound of my heart.
My heart has a new love again,
A true love,
A love that gives like no other.

I will enjoy every waking moment.
My life has begun, is everyone in?
That show is about to begin!

Elaine W.

# Cracks in Our Walls

Walls are everywhere.
The building has walls,
Each room within has walls,
Every person inside these rooms has walls.

It seems we all have a common goal,
To knock down our walls.
It sounds so easy,
It rolls off the tongue as if a breath could tumble them.
The reality is that it took us years to fortify these walls,
These walls that keep us safe.
It is terrifying to imagine living without them.

It reminds me of ancient cities.
The inhabitants would construct walls to encompass the entire city.
If they were attacked,
This colossal wall would protect them.
It often took years to build the walls to maximum security.
When enemies would attack, they may chip rock
Or break small pieces of the wall,
Yet the wall remained—if perhaps a little weaker.
Over time the walls became weaker and weaker,
Weaker with each battle.
Eventually, the walls would slowly crumble.

So, we must remember that it took time to strengthen our walls,
Our walls that protect us from pain.
But we can persist in putting cracks in these walls,
We can break them one piece at a time and they, too will crumble.
Then we will be free to live!

Jennifer G.

# Confused

I'm lost, angry and confused,
Hurting, empty and sad.
But I'm happy at the same time.
I really want this program to work for me,
Because if it doesn't, I'm going to die.

If I was ever to go back,
It would ruin all of my work,
All that I have done to be sober.

Today I am so grateful to be here.
I cannot wait to go to meetings and to start exercising.
It's a pain having to get up in the morning,
But in the end it's worth it.
I love the ladies I'm living with,
Even though I can't stand living with people.

I miss my boys so much.
I miss my boyfriend and friends, too.
But I know if I don't stay,
I won't have anyone in my life and that would kill me.
I want to find direction,
Find out where to go or what to do next.
It takes time, I know, but it will happen.

Crystal R.

# I Wake and Breathe the Morning Air

I wake and breathe the morning air.
When I wake up in a good mood, I open my bedroom window,
I hear the birds chirping up in their nests,
I see the squirrels shaking their bushy tails,
I see the tree branches blowing back and forth.

I wake and breathe the morning air.
Sometimes when I wake it's raining
And it puts me in a sad mood.
It's not a good day for walking,
But it helps the beautiful flowers and the shiny green grass to grow.
And at the end of the rainy day,
You can see a beautiful rainbow,
With the colours red, orange, yellow, green, blue, purple.

Nicole S.

# Round and Round

We need power to make the world go round,
Although sometimes power does not make a sound.
Round and round in our little world it goes,
Stopping for nothing, not even our woes.
The next turn ahead seems so far,
Give me, oh please, the power of a star.
Put behind me fears and doubt,
In myself, I am devout.
Clarity of mind gives me power,
Words of the truth in this final hour.

Lynne M.

# The One Who's There With Me!

Father,
The one who truly knows me,
The only thing that I won't stop believing in,
I won't give in to letting go.
The strength that's given by him, my higher power,
It's the only thing I believe in.
I will never stop praying,
Praying for the will to be able to speak to my one and only soul,
The only breath I've ever felt in such a beautiful way.
And that's the reason I'm here today.
Thank you, my higher power.

Tanya W.

# A Part of Me

When I woke this morning,
My startle reflexes kicked in.
Bang, bang, bang.
Wake up! It's 7 a.m.
Oh God.
Why? Why? Why?
Do I conform?
A park bench is where I want to be,
Yet I am here.
His dark, evil, drug-induced look flashes in my mind,
The tears catch in my throat.

Where is my coffee? No cream.
Where is my comfort?
Where are my two hours of morning solitude?

Her shrill, brash voice irks me.
Shut up, new girl! Shut up!
I hiss in response.
My lips betray my mind.
She sounds just like me when I was her age.
I shut my eyes,
Praying for peace.

Coffee at last,
My hands envelope the mug,
Savouring the warmth
Ah, yeah.

My mind drifts to my birthday,
The Beanermunkey chocolates,
The chaos and melodrama that followed.

All I wanted was someone to be nice to me.
How I long for my lover
And a long passionate soul stare over a cappuccino conversation,
A world I shrunk away from for so long.

Later I find myself at Jackson's Square surrounded by the evolved people,
The living, breathing, wall of people.
I am part of the shopping people,
The people who care about the one hundred mile diet.
I am a part of the human race today.

I hum a tune in my soul,
My smile showing my thoughts, no fear.
I dream of my return,
I am valid with no money today,
My validation is no longer sought externally.
My courage sustains me,
Nourishes my body, mind and spirit.
Nagging thoughts intrude swiftly,
I push them away.
Onwards and upwards,
You go girl!
Home sweet home
Will be mine soon enough.
The coffee will be served any way you like it, honey.

April A.

# The Power That Drives Me

The task ahead is never as great as the power behind us.
And what a power it is that drives us forward with so much pain and
determination.
The task ahead seems so small,
The power so great,
But the time so short.
Power is something I have never lacked,
But great decision making is.
The power that drives me today is fueled by my strength to survive,
My desire to keep going,
And all the mistakes I have made in my short life.
But this is my power and my fate,
For I deserve to be happy
And finish whatever task I set for myself.
I can do anything with my power,
I can accomplish anything I put my mind to.
Sobriety has shown me that my power is greater when I have a clear
mind.
The torture I put myself and others through during my addiction was not
in vain,
For I have learned from every experience.
Every tear that I shed
And every heart that I broke was for a reason.
That reason and this power brought me here,
Where I am today,
Clean, clear and focused,
Focused on the task at hand,
And with all the power I need to fulfill my desires.

Jessica M.

# When I Go Out Into The World

When I go out into the world,
I want to be great, feel great,
And do amazing things.

I've been out in the bad part of the world,
Where it's dark, cold and lonely.
I was always chasing,
Chasing the drugs,
The bad people in my life.

Now I want to go out,
Out into the rest of the world,
Where there's colour and happy people,
People who make me happy,
Who inspire me,
Who encourage me to do great things.

When I go out into the world,
I'm going to be scared,
But I will be happy,
Scared because it's the unknown
But happy because it's new and no longer dark.

When I go out into the world,
I want to learn how I can help others,
So I can show them that they can go out into the rest of the world too.
When I go out into the world,
I want to explore,
Explore everything and every place that is good.

When I go out into the world,
I will be clean and sober,
With clear blue eyes.

Taisha A.

# Riding the Road Into the Spring

Riding the road into spring,
Where do I go from here?
Riding the road into spring,
I'm lost.

I wait for the season with anticipation,
Yet I worry where I will be.

I look forward to the coming of spring,
It means I have lived to see another one.

I fear I will be no further ahead.

I love spring.
The coldness is gone,
It always makes me feel more alive.

I hope it is better this time,
I would like to enjoy it as I used to.
My days have become a blur,
One day just like the other.

I know I can change,
This will be the year,
Riding the road into spring.

Sarah H.

# Get Your Ass Off the Table

When I woke up this morning,
I felt I didn't want to wake up!
But when I walked out of the room,
I looked at the wall and saw the kid's pictures,
Looking back at me.
I knew it was time to get up,
Time to start my way into rehab.

My first day May 30, 2011!
My daughter told me to get my ass moving,
Get my butt in gear and get going!
Go Mommy, Mommy go!
Once you're done this, Mommy,
We can come back home and all be a family again!

My mom once told me that tables are for glasses, not asses.
So get your ass off the table,
Get to rehab,
Because I want my family back,
I want to be a big sister to my baby brother.

Please, Mommy, please!

So, here I am,
Here I go,
On my journey of recovery.
I've never been so excited to start.

Karrie S.

# Less Than Perfect

I am determined to fight for my survival.

Please don't judge.

It's been a ride to say the least.

Yeah, I hung myself.
Yeah, I cut myself.
Yeah, I drank myself stupid.
Yeah, I stood on the edge of a bridge.
Yeah, I was in jail.
Yeah, I did drugs.
Yeah, I was raped.
Yeah, I was beaten.
Yeah, I overdosed.
Yeah, I almost died.

I've got more than nine lives, I guess.

So here comes the kicker:
I crawled out of that hole,
Planted my feet on the ground,
Asked myself why?
What have I done?
I was so lost inside.

I should of guessed what it was coming to.

Sitting in a hospital bed with a breathing tube down my throat,
I awoke from this drug-induced coma.
Demons were haunting me like the devil on your shoulder and that was it.
I hit bottom for the very last time.
I was determined to fight for my survival,
And I did.

This is me.
I'm a survivor 'til the end

It hurt so bad,
I wanted to die.
And I tried.
But now I believe there is some purpose,
Some reason I'm not dead.
My life has become my own.
I'm learning, listening,
I'm living.

I know for whatever reason
I had to endure all the pain I caused myself
To let the light pour in and bring me the truth
When the time was right.

I now consider myself an equal.
I'm a person who matters,
A person who deserves more in life.
I now understand that it was always there,
But I was blinded.

So now every minute, every second
Is a work in progress for me.

I can go as slow or as fast as I want or need.
This is how my life will be

But I will fight for my survival while I'm still here.
I want to live.
I want to be a good person.
And it's only little old me who calls the shots.
Today, tomorrow and for the rest of my life.

Alessandra B.

# We have earned our Chair

Sitting with women in recovery.
Writing with women in recovery.
Something so safe, our common bond,
Fodder for exploration, creativity.
We have each earned our chair, our right to voice.

I'm allowed to be here . . .

Michelle V.

# Time to Be Free

My world could be amazing
If I let myself be free,
Free of all the turmoil
And the addiction that captures me.
I'm begging to take the right steps,
To free my troubled head.
I'm taking an honest look at myself.
I'll make a brand new start.
I'll make the right choices,
Seeking guidance when I'm blue.
I'm making my life my own again,
Because that's what I need to do.

Dianna D.

# Goodbye My Friend

You have been there in my time of need.
You have been my very best friend for most of my life.
You have comforted me when I was sad,
You have helped me when I was angry,
You have taken away my loneliness,
You have celebrated with me when I was happy.

But there came a time you took control of me.
You stopped comforting me,
You stripped me of my dignity,
You stripped me of my identity.

I believed you were helping me,
I believed I was making the decisions,
But instead you were the one who was manipulating me.
How I acted, the lies to cover lies,
The mind games that you played,
They were all to keep me in your grasp.

You have abused me,
You made me ill,
And I lost my will to go on without you.
You were in every aspect of my life,
You promised me heaven
And all you gave me was hell.
I gave you everything—my kids, my family,
Anything I had,
And I was left an empty shell.

Now I have taken my life back,
There is no room for you.

Goodbye.
You are no friend of mine.

Kim M.

# Where I'm At

Where the wild things are, everyone's perspective is different.
What is wild to them isn't wild to me,
Because I think of myself as a wild person at times,
Letting my world get out of hand,
Being the one who is always getting hurt,
And I'm the only one to blame.
But somewhere deep down inside me,
I want to put the blame on someone else.
It's very confusing for me,
Not understanding myself.
Why am I always causing pain to myself?
It doesn't make too much sense.
All I want is to stop hurting myself,
So then maybe I'll stop hurting my loved ones,
The ones that are always in my life,
Especially now,
Because I have managed to bring a wonderful,
Pure, beautiful little boy into this world.
He doesn't deserve to be treated in those ways
Or to have any extra pain—that's all my doing,
All because of me being selfish,
Too scared to stand up for my true wants and desires,
The things that I really deserve.
I think I just need to open my eyes,
Step out of my comfort zone for once,
And truly believe.

Tanya W.

# A Moment of Clarity

In my moment of hesitation,
I had a serious revelation,
That came to a contemplation of thought.
No longer lost and distraught,
A new path now sought,
My soul I brought back,
And that's a fact!

Kim R.

# Victorious

When I go out into the world,
No longer do I keep my head bowed
and my eyes to the ground,
Wandering out mostly at night,
Preyed upon by cops and despicable spite.
I'm expendable in society's eyes,
The sudden hate catches me by surprise.

These days are brighter,
But I'm still a fighter.
My battles are a new challenge.
With each day I bear,
I am more aware
of my victorious stance—
Head up, eyes open,
No longer broken.

Anonymous

# Clean and Sober

Clean and sober,
That you are.
Stay that way,
And you'll go far.
But if you feel like falling down,
Use some tools
And you'll come 'round.

Laura Y.

# The Trek

Although the time is nearly done,
It seems the battle has been won.
I know I still have work to do,
A thank you, though, from me to you.
The tools you all have armed me with
I'll take with me as facts not myth
As I re-join society
And embrace my sobriety.

Karon B.

# I'm Free

Freedom from addiction,
So glad I'm free.
One day at a time.
I feel so free inside
I can fly,
Just like a dragonfly.
What a feeling inside,
I'm free.

I'm so free.
Looking at the flowers, trees, fresh air,
I am so pretty and colourful inside.
I can go anywhere,
See the birds, the water, the blue sky.
I am so free, and I love it.
I'm free.

My insides have butterflies.
Everything is so beautiful.
No matter what way I go,
I'm free.

I'm free one day at a time,
I love myself for staying clean,
I'm free.

I'm free,
Just fly away anywhere,
I'm free.

Laureen R.

# About the Photographer

Studying photography at Sheridan College, Carolyn discovered she had a true gift. Her photos are haunting and gorgeous. They tell stories. Her work is even more impressive when one discovers Carolyn has been blind in one eye since she was a toddler. A true survivor, Carolyn is proud to acknowledge the battles she has waged with concurrent disorders: borderline personality disorder, depression, alcoholism, disassociation disorder and severe agoraphobia. She believes her art has helped her survive and she is passionate about sharing her story so that others can learn they are not alone.

# About our Back Cover Painting
## by April Anderson

April created this work of art to show that out of great pain comes great beauty. Her attitude about life is no matter the obstacle, there is always something you can do to take yourself to a better place. Perhaps, she says it best in her own words: "Nobody really has God on speed dial But if I did, He would tell me to get out and push."